Life Doesn't
Get Any Better
Than This

Life Doesn't Get Any Better Than This

The Holiness
of Little Daily Dramas

ROBERT A. ALPER

LIGUORI/TRIUMPH
LIGUORI, MISSOURI

Published by Liguori/Triumph
An Imprint of Liguori Publications
Liguori, Missouri
http://www.liguori.org

Library of Congress Cataloging-in-Publication Data

Alper, Robert A. (Robert Abelson)
   Life doesn't get any better than this : the holiness of little daily
dramas / Robert A. Alper.—1st ed.
      p. cm.
   ISBN 0-89243-932-7
   1. Ethics, Jewish. 2. Jewish parables. 3. Jews—Anecdotes. I.
Title.
BJ1287.A55183   1996
296.1'9—dc20   96–12887

The poem "Birth Is a Beginning" by Rabbi Alvin I. Fine excerpted
from *Gates of Repentance*, copyright 1978 by the Central Conference of American Rabbis and the Union of Liberal and Progressive
Synagogues. Reprinted by permission.

Printed in the United States of America
03 02 01 00 99   8 7 6 5 4

To Sherri

She speaks with a gentle wisdom
And the teaching of kindness is on her lips.

Proverbs 31:26

I always thought authors sounded just a bit pretentious when they wrote about "finding their voices" ... until I had the very good fortune to work with the perceptive literary agent Denise Marcil, who sensed some potential in me and helped me find my voice. Denise is one of the people who gently guided me, the others being Joan Marlow Golan and Pat Kossmann of Triumph Books, sensitive, insightful mentors who gracefully choreographed the delicate dance of writer and co-editors. Special thanks to close friends Rabbi Leigh Lerner and my comedy manager, Sherry Goodman, for their encouragement along the way.

Birth is a beginning
And death a destination.
And life is a journey:
From childhood to maturity
And youth to age;
From innocence to awareness
And ignorance to knowing;
From foolishness to discretion
    And then, perhaps, to wisdom;
From weakness to strength
Or strength to weakness—
    And, often, back again;
From health to sickness
    And back, we pray, to health again;
From offense to forgiveness,
From loneliness to love,
From joy to gratitude,
From pain to compassion,
And grief to understanding—
    From fear to faith;
From defeat to defeat to defeat—
Until, looking backward or ahead,
We see that victory lies
Not at some high place along the way,
But in having made the journey, stage by stage,
    A sacred pilgrimage.
Birth is a beginning
And death a destination.
And life is a journey,
A sacred pilgrimage—
    To life everlasting.

—Rabbi Alvin I. Fine
from *Gates of Repentance*, p. 283.

Contents

God and the Taxi Driver: An Introduction   1

Part I
BIRTH IS A BEGINNING
AND DEATH A DESTINATION

1. *Angel of Birth*   8

2. *Holding, Loving, and Letting Go*   13

3. *The Moment of Death*   17

4. *Remembering John*   20

Part II
FROM CHILDHOOD TO MATURITY
AND YOUTH TO AGE

5. *Afghans*   28

6. *A Private Ceremony*   35

7. *Shadowed Celebrations*   41

8. *Moments of Connection*   44

Part III
FROM INNOCENCE TO AWARENESS
AND IGNORANCE TO KNOWING

9. *The Blink of an Eye*   50

10. *I'd Give Anything ... Anything*   54

11. *December Memories* 60

12. *Lust and Love* 65

Part IV
FROM FOOLISHNESS TO DISCRETION
AND THEN, PERHAPS, TO WISDOM

13. *The Toll* 72

14. *The Doctors of Ministry* 80

15. *Humanity 101* 86

Part V
FROM WEAKNESS TO STRENGTH
OR STRENGTH TO WEAKNESS

16. *Unlikely Hero* 92

17. *Mittens and Gloves* 97

18. *What Really Matters* 100

Part VI
FROM HEALTH TO SICKNESS
AND BACK, WE PRAY, TO HEALTH AGAIN

19. *Getting Unstuck* 106

20. *Thank Heaven for Wisdom Teeth* 114

21. *To Baby, with Love* 119

Part VII
FROM OFFENSE TO FORGIVENESS

22. *The Parable of the Knee*	126
23. *A Second Chance*	129
24. *Our Neighbor, Everyone's Friend*	134
25. *The Saxophone Player*	139

Part VIII
FROM LONELINESS TO LOVE

26. *A Woman Named Elizabeth Badt*	146
27. *A Child Comes Home*	149
28. *Between Father and Son*	156

Part IX
FROM JOY TO GRATITUDE

29. *Life Doesn't Get Any Better than This*	162
30. *The Glance*	167
31. *A Holy Privilege*	170

Part X
FROM PAIN TO COMPASSION
AND GRIEF TO UNDERSTANDING

32. *A Mother and a Daughter*	176
33. *Old Lovers*	183
34. *A Welcome Stranger*	187

Part XI
FROM FEAR TO FAITH

35. *Choosing a Different Path*   192

36. *The Rabbi/Stand-Up Comic*   194

37. *The Man Who Was "Not Religious"*   200

Part XII
FROM DEFEAT TO DEFEAT TO DEFEAT...
UNTIL VICTORY

38. *Transcending Murphy's Law*   206

39. *Gerda's Gift*   211

40. *Fraternal Recognition*   219

Part XIII
LIFE IS A JOURNEY

41. *Departures*   226

42. *Taking Yourself Lightly*   231

43. *Reincarnating (Sort of) the Dead*   234

44. *Two Lives, Two Triumphs*   240

God and the Taxi Driver: An Introduction

"Phew! He's making a U-turn. I think we got him."

One of those windy, rainy nights in New York City when a person's love for all humanity skips just a beat via the thought, "Puh-leeze let that cab stop for us, and not them...."

We're in luck. The big yellow Dodge eases toward us. We back away, expecting a splash of water, but there is none, only an unhurried approach to the piece of sidewalk we'd staked out. Close enough to the curb so we can all bundle into the vehicle without sloshing through the puddle.

I announce our destination through the holes in the safety shield that separates driver from passengers, and then silently try to read the name on the identification card. Too many consonants, too few vowels. I give up and resume a discussion I'd been having with my companions.

Our cab zigzags down Broadway, keeping pace with traffic but without the heroics — or idiocy — displayed by other vehicles. Occasionally we are cut off, and once nearly sideswiped by a bus changing lanes. Our driver grits his teeth but holds his temper. Politely, with difficulty, he tries to answer our questions and engage in simple conversation. This is how he is learning English, he explains.

We reach our destination. The others pile out of the taxi and run under the awning, while I fumble for my wallet. Trying to use simple words, I compliment the driver on his skills, telling him how we had all just eaten a big meal (I pat my stomach) and that a bumpy ride could have caused us to "lose" some of our food (another gesture). He understands, and we both laugh. I pay him, including a large tip. He thanks me and drives off. Slowly, without splashing.

— ❖ —

I love to tell stories. Even stories about this cabdriver, who will reappear at the end of this chapter. Jews love to tell stories, and much of our people's wisdom is passed along in such a manner. That's sometimes hard for others to understand. A simple explanation is the fact that Jews differ from many other groups in that for many of us, matters of belief, faith, theology, have always been implicit and taken for granted, while matters regarding a person's actions in both religious and secular affairs have always received the closest attention. My favorite explanation of how faith and behavior come into play in a Jew's life is Rabbi Yitzchak Greenberg's wry definition of a Jewish atheist: "One who knows what the God in whom he does not believe expects of him"!

But I do feel that I owe the reader a theological word or two at the outset in order to explain why certain commonly used "God talk" may be absent in these essays, while at the same time, I hope a sense of God infuses the book.

One's history informs one's theology. I was born to Jewish parents in January 1945. Fortunately, a couple of generations earlier, people named Alper and Abelson and Lewinsohn and Katzenstein took a risk, piled onto boats, and came to a place called America. It could have been different. I could have been born elsewhere.

Elsewhere was Europe, at a time when "ordinary" men spent their days heaving living Jewish children into bonfires, and then returned to their homes, played with their sons and daughters, ate a pleasant evening meal, and listened to fine music.

I simply cannot say, "This was God's will." "This was all

part of God's unfathomable plan." Nor can I make similar statements when I think of the Cambodian genocide, the horrors of Rwanda, or the rape of Bosnia.

Others, even very wise people, may disagree. And I respond, "You may be right. I make no claim to having the absolute truth."

Quite honestly, I worry about those who feel they know the absolute truth in matters religious. After all, with what does religion concern itself? With themes that are beyond science, beyond empirical proof, such as the nature of God, what constitutes ethical behavior, the value of rituals, and questions of existence after death.

I have no absolute answers. (As for those who think they do, I hope they will respect me and leave me alone.)

The fact is, the majority of Jews are liberal, and in our diverse community there are many theological opinions coexisting rather well. On the nature of God, for example.

Some consider God an internal force that propels a person to do good. Some see God as a humanlike being who is all-good, all-powerful, all-knowing, and capable of being addressed through prayer. Some see God as the first cause of the universe who no longer interferes in human affairs. And some find meaning in the kind of finite theism described by Rabbi Harold Kushner in his book *When Bad Things Happen to Good People:* a God who is all-knowing, all-benevolent, but not all-powerful; a God who cannot work miracles or change nature but is humanity's friend and helper and source of determination, vision, and courage.

As for me, I absolutely love being a Jew, being part of the Jewish people. As my life's experiences roll forward, I am grateful for the freedom to learn, and grow, and evolve. I'm not finished yet.

Where am I now? Well, first of all, I believe there is a

God, because on various occasions I've heard babies giggle. That's proof enough for me. But if I need any further confirmation, all I need to do is look outside my window, at the mountains of my beloved Vermont. I'm a very fortunate fellow, living in a place where a trip to the general store provides scenery that can, and often does, bring tears to my eyes. Mountains are humbling. Ennobling. Inspiring.

I can't believe that babies giggle because of a cosmic accident. I believe a baby's sound is a divine creation, as are the mountains and all else in the universe.

With creation comes potential, each moment influencing the next, each act helping construct the future. My teacher Rabbi Alvin Reines calls it "the enduring possibility of being," and suggests we relate to God in the way we affect that next second of the universe's existence. Like the rays of the sun, emanating from a central source, stretching for miles and miles until they reach earth: We can choose to allow the rays to warm the ground, or block the energy, or refract it away in a different direction.

As for human beings, our every word, our every action, for good or for evil, positive or negative, has a bearing on that ongoing act of creation. And defines our connection with God.

All of which brings us back to the taxi driver.

In my imagination I envisioned that the story may have continued in this way: Because I complimented the driver, gave him a chuckle, and presented him with a generous tip, his evening ended pleasurably. The next day, more refreshed than usual, he spent some extra time with his eight-year-old daughter, raising her sense of self-esteem. And because of the support she received from her father, this child will now confidently realize her potential, becoming a research scientist and ultimately developing a serum that will eradicate cancer forever.

Far-fetched? Of course! Possible? Sure. And reason enough, in my view, to place ultimate importance on each and every one of our actions. When a stone is tossed into a pond, the ripples spread outward in all directions, eventually becoming invisible, but with movement and energy steadily stretching outward nevertheless. Our behavior, too, continually touches and influences the future as we assume our roles in that ongoing act of creation.

And so, one might then ask, where can God be found in these stories?

My hope is, everywhere.

– I –

Birth Is a Beginning
and Death a Destination

1. Angel of Birth

"Let's take a vote," I suggested. "Secret ballot. We'll keep it honest."

My wife and I sat on opposite sides of the wobbly metal card table that practically filled our apartment's tiny breakfast room. Dinner was over, and we found ourselves once again mulling over the pros and the cons. This was no minor issue. It was the most important decision a man and woman can make, and while we approached the topic joyfully, we were serious about critical related concerns such as timing and finances.

Were we ready to start a family?

Sherri and I had been married for two years, living the "genteel poverty" lifestyle of a graduate student and a severely underemployed wife. In ten months, though, I would be ordained as a rabbi, entering my profession at a time when there were several positions available for every new ordinee. Both of us were young and healthy, and we adored kids.

Still, the idea of beginning a family, of creating a life, is an awesome notion. By now we were weary of the months of discussions, projections, and, mostly, dreaming. But neither wanted to pressure the other, and so we agreed to decide in a strictly democratic fashion. One vote per person. Secret ballots. No fair peeking at what the other was writing.

Two sharp pencils. Two pieces of paper of equal size. High drama as empty supper plates were slid out of the way and cupped hands shielded the words being scratched on the small white squares.

We folded our ballots in parallel syncopation. I nominated myself to read the results, and Sherri seconded the nomination. Tension. I opened the first ballot to discover my own handwriting, and following a dramatic pause declared, "It says 'Yes!'" Applause.

On to the remaining ballot. I cleverly deduced that it was Sherri's. Slowly, carefully, I opened one fold, then the other, finally grasping the paper between the thumb and index finger of both hands.

She had written, "John Kennedy."

Ten months later, and precisely six days before my ordination, our son was born.

God, we were lucky.

– ❖ –

The initial hints of labor began while we were taking a walk on a Saturday afternoon. We started timing the contractions mid-evening, and at about 1:00 A.M. decided it was time to proceed to the hospital. It was only a two- or three-mile drive, but I distinctly remember heading south on Reading Road behind a slow-moving truck, thinking, mentally shouting, "Get out of the way! My wife's having a baby!"

And, of course, she did. After an additional fifteen hours of labor.

Once we completed the admissions paperwork, Sherri was taken to her room to be "prepped," and I was directed to the maternity ward waiting area. Only a temporary separation, I knew, since we had graduated with honors from the "husband-coached natural childbirth" classes and planned to be together throughout the entire experience. I spent about an hour in that dreadful alcove, occasionally watching a soundless black-and-white version of *The Nun's Story* playing across a television set anchored to a high wall. Three older women from rural Kentucky sat nearby, passing the time one-upping each other with stories of power lawn-mower accidents. I did not contribute.

Around 2:30 A.M. they finally let me enter Sherri's room. We assumed we were into the home stretch, and that within an hour or two everything would be over. During the next thirteen hours we learned more about labor than they ever taught us in the classes.

This was 1972, a transitional era in childbirth protocols. For the first time some fathers were allowed to attend the birth of their children, subject to two requirements, one smart and one stupid. The men were obligated to attend a full set of childbirth-education classes. Excellent, sensible idea. But if the mother needed to take any kind of pain medication, if the birth was to be anything other than completely "natural," the father was banished to the waiting area. A patently dumb rule that would be rescinded some time later.

We were bound by the existing regulations. And so, hour after hour, Sherri courageously refused medication, determined that we should be together for the anticipated moment of holiness, the birth of our child.

The obstetrician arrived. I donned my scrub suit. But there were complications. Finally, reluctantly, for the sake of our child's well-being, Sherri accepted her doctor's recommendation that she take a mild pain killer. I remained by her side during those final minutes of labor, and then we were instructed to say good-bye as Sherri was hustled off to the delivery room and I was invited to wait in the lobby.

And that's when she appeared. An angel.

I hadn't really noticed her before. I think she must have just joined the nursing team after the 3:00 P.M. shift change. A tall black woman in a green uniform, she broke away from the procession escorting Sherri along the corridor and nodded in my direction.

"Come with me," she whispered. "As long as nobody

notices you, you can stand in the supply room. There's a window in the door, and you can see into the delivery area." I arrived at my post just as they wheeled Sherri in.

Soon after I began my vigil, the angel entered the supply room, grabbed some small object, and then "forgot" to close the door. My view from fifteen feet was obstructed most of the time by the doctor and nurses, but Sherri could see me in between her pushes, and while she didn't smile, there was a glimmer of relief in our quick, silent eye conversations.

The team was fully engaged. *It won't be long now.* The angel backed away from the delivery table, eyes on the doctor, one hand behind her waist, holding a surgical mask. When she reached me, she turned her head to the side and murmured over her shoulder, "Here. Put this on." Then the hand that had held the mask began to beckon to me, instructing me to follow her large figure closely as she edged nearer and nearer to where Sherri lay.

I ended up standing right next to the obstetrician as he helped our baby emerge. No, I couldn't hold Sherri's hand or cradle her head during the critical moments as I'd hoped to do. But we were able to look directly into each other's eyes, sometimes clearly, mostly through the glistening fog of joyful tears. That was just as nice. And together we watched as our son was born.

We thanked the doctor and the nurses. Briefly. They had another birth to attend, and our lives had been monumentally transformed. That's the way things happen in busy maternity units. We never saw the angel again. Never even learned her name.

It's amazing. This stranger entered our lives for the briefest time, possibly risked her job, and enabled us to share that exquisite moment of life's beginning, when every prayer has been answered and every dream is still a possibility. Then she turned to another assignment, another woman in labor, another baby about to be born.

Having made a lifetime's difference for us, she moved on to her next task. And we, overwhelmed, exhausted, nervously holding God's most precious gift, began to make our telephone calls.

2. Holding, Loving, and Letting Go

The soap operas, I'm convinced, would never touch a story like this one.

Even *ER* and *Chicago Hope* with their mini-epidemics and javelins-through-the-chest and bloody surgical catastrophes would shy away from such a subject.

Too depressing. Much too depressing. And besides, viewers would probably think it was overly contrived, not realistic, too melodramatic.

Yet it actually happened, one of the quiet, unreported incidents that occur every day in hospitals and, in their own way, teach lessons and lend new understanding about the nature of life and love and purpose.

It was a crisis in the maternity ward of a small hospital. Not an emergency. No crash carts or shouting of rapid-fire orders or heroic, inventive surgery. But a crisis nevertheless. A quiet crisis.

A young woman, perhaps twenty years old, sat silently in the stuffed chair in her room, staring off into space, holding, hugging, the baby she had recently delivered. The little boy, suffering from a congenital heart defect, had been born alive but died shortly afterward. There was nothing that could be done to save his life.

In order to help the mother in her grief, the doctor and nurses had dressed the child, wrapped him in a soft blanket, and placed him in his mother's arms, a way of giving her an opportunity to say good-bye to that which had been a part of her for nine months. It was also a way for her at least to begin to say good-bye to the dreams and plans that are part of bearing a child.

The mother and son spent some minutes alone together, and then a nurse approached, gently suggesting that the time had come to surrender the baby. The mother was reluctant, then adamant. "No, not yet. I'm not ready to give him up." The nurse acquiesced. But minutes became hours, and eventually a wrenching situation became a crisis.

It lasted for two days.

Nurses, doctors, and a few visitors all attempted to reason with the mother, to convince her to let go of the child. Throughout the hospital the standoff became the major topic of discussion, with many people offering their solutions. Some suggested using force, others recommended a stealthily administered tranquilizer. The mood of the staff, usually efficiently, encouragingly upbeat, now mirrored the grim, stagnant scene in that maternity ward. The dreadful drama seemed to go on forever.

Finally, a clinical social worker was called for a consultation. Cautiously the woman entered the room, introduced herself, and admired the tiny child, still held closely in the mother's arms. The two spoke for quite a while, until a level of trust had been established. At that point the social worker asked if she might hold the baby, just for a minute. Only a minute. The mother warily agreed. The social worker took the child, and a minute later returned him to the mother.

Later, the same request. "May I hold him again?" The mother, more trusting, now parted with him for three minutes, then five, then ten. At last the social worker and the mother agreed: It was time to say a final good-bye. As if performing a sacred ritual, the social worker took a teddy bear from the nearby windowsill, wrapped it in the baby's blanket, and placed it in the mother's arms in exchange for the child. The mother hugged the bear and sobbed softly as the baby was taken from the room.

When I heard this story, I wondered, first of all, why the mother held on to the baby so tenaciously, in an almost macabre way. And more important, I wondered, as I often do, about the meaning of the short life of that baby.

The social worker helped me understand by providing some additional details. This was the mother's first child, and she was a person who was virtually alone. The child's father was not in the picture at all, and the woman had grown up in a home where she was ignored, unappreciated, unloved. From the moment the child was born and throughout the unfolding drama, this young woman found herself the object of care, compassion, sympathy, empathy. It was not an egotistical adventure. It was a painful situation but also, simply, surprisingly, one in which, for the very first time, the woman became the center of attention and was receiving the kind of stroking we all need.

She did not want to let go of her baby. And she did not want to let go of this very new role in which people attended her, commiserated with her, and most helpful of all, even cried with her.

And what of the baby?

Various religions and philosophies would attempt to explain the baby's existence in radically different ways. Some people speak with complete authority, they the possessors of absolute truth, while others offer educated speculation based on experience, intuition, and faith. The infant's life, so brief, is a prelude to an eternity as one of God's special beloved, some might declare. Others anticipate a resurrection, or some variety of reincarnation, or an absolute, final end at death. And still others simply brand such speculation as irrelevant; since we cannot know for certain what transpires after death, our psychic energies might be better spent examining and improving the earthly life we experience every day.

Yet, despite theological disagreements, I believe all persons would concur that the child's tragically short life had some ultimate meaning. His contribution to the ongoing human drama was significant: Because of this baby, for at least forty-eight hours a young woman who never knew love felt loved. For two days a young woman, emotionally neglected throughout her life, was the object of concern, her feelings valued, her sorrow shared.

Life is full of mystery, from the unknown dimensions of the expanding universe to the quiet tragedies and victories that take place every day in likely and unlikely places.

An autumn afternoon. A pallid young woman rises slowly from her wheelchair, smiles sadly, appreciatively, to the orderly and to the social worker. She enters the taxi. Alone.

In her arms she cradles a teddy bear, wrapped in a baby's blanket.

3. The Moment of Death

Following the birth of our son, when the doctor had given us the wonderful news of the good health of mother and child, and Sherri relaxed into well-earned sleep, I left the hospital to return to our apartment. Squinting in the sunlight, I fully expected that somehow the world would be different, that somehow things would have changed dramatically and drastically.

But of course not very much had changed. The buses still spewed forth diesel fumes, the afternoon traffic was burdened with the same congestion, pleasant people smiled, sad people frowned, and the world was the same.

I recalled that experience a few years later when I had the privilege — and it really was a profound privilege — to be present at the moment of death of a remarkable man.

After so many months of a courageous struggle against a disease he knew he could never defeat, after so many months of pain that he encountered with incredible strength, his life gradually ebbed away until the final hours when he lay in a coma.

What was the difference between life and death? During his final hours life was peaceful. Death, when it came, was more peaceful. What was the difference between life and death? Not a sigh, not a movement, not even a whisper. Only peace.

All manners of dying, all deaths, are unique, some without pain, many with great suffering. And the timing of death is often so cruel. Sometimes in the fullness of years, sometimes long before one's life song is finished, sometimes in the innocence of youth; and there are some deaths — a miscarriage, a stillborn child — for which we do not even truly know how to mourn, though the pain is severe and lasting.

But the end of a life, a death, no matter how it occurs, means a final and eternal peace.

After our friend died, after we tenderly closed his eyes and recited the Twenty-third Psalm, after these rituals had been completed, I realized that the room had suddenly been bathed in holiness.

His eyeglasses, resting on the bedside stand and never to be used again, had become a holy object. So, too, the half-full glass of water with its straw, the unfinished book, the pencil, the paper, the watch, and everything surrounding that only moments before had been servants to a living being — all of these for now, for a brief or even long time, had become holy vessels.

But these objects were not only repositories of holiness. As I looked around the room, I realized that this same holiness, in a very important way, had attached itself to the people who had shared in that moment of death.

Immediately, only seconds after the death, a new world began to unfold in which the people whose lives he had touched began to assume the proud and noble task of assuring his immortality through the perpetuation of his memory, the perpetuation of his spirit, his courage, his warmth, his gentleness, and his love.

What is the difference between life and death? Not even a sigh, not even a soft whisper. Only peace.

I left that house at two o'clock in the morning and, as had happened years before, I was amazed to realize that the world continued to flow even though he was no longer among us. The moon was bright. People slept in their houses. Cats scurried about, and an occasional bird called against the summer breeze.

Could the world continue to go on without him? It could. It does.

Could his family go on without him? They can. They do.

And they will, with melancholy pain and profound sorrow, but also with a stirring challenge to live their lives as he did and to honor his memory through lofty thoughts and compassionate deeds.

The death of a loved one robs us of joy, of pleasure, of security, but death need not rob us of the resolve to find satisfaction in the years left to us, and we *must* not allow death to rob us of the belief that our world can still be beautiful.

Our friend's moment of death was awesome even as it was gentle. We entered a new realm of existence, we survivors, the moment death came. His life was now totality, a completeness to be summarized and evaluated. He died, and we then were able to reaffirm what we knew all along: that his life had been one of majesty.

Death: for this sweet man, not a whisper, not a sigh; only the crossing over of a very thin, nearly hidden threshold. To peacefulness.

4. Remembering John

I guess I knew that someday I'd find myself writing about John.

I knew it ever since the moment I learned that he had died. Writing is my therapy, my way of trying to think things out, to figure things out.

Only, I thought that by the time I started to write about his loss, about my pain — I thought that by this time I'd have answers, solutions, explanations.

Instead, all I have are the same questions, the same bewilderment that I tried to confront at the time of his death. I should have known that answers come very slowly, if at all.

What I have found is that even if answers never come, asking the questions, sharing the sadness and the confusion, is helpful. Very helpful.

His name was John Walter. Forty-eight years old. Married to Carolyn, father of Kim and Brian. Born on a Lancaster, Pennsylvania, farm. Lived in Swarthmore, Pennsylvania, near Philadelphia. John was a lawyer's lawyer, even serving for a few years as dean of students at Temple University's Law School. Later he became a partner at a firm called Marshall Dennehey.

Sherri and Carolyn became friends while attending the Bryn Mawr Graduate School of Social Work. John and I sort of fell into line, as husbands sometimes do. It wasn't an intense friendship — we lived forty-five minutes away from each other until moving to Vermont — but it was a special friendship, born of mutual life experiences, and nurtured by significant mileposts along the way.

Carolyn and I were born on the very same day. Kim is a year older than our son, Zack, and Brian is a year older than our daughter, Jessie. Our families mixed well, vacationed together.

After we moved to Vermont, I continued to conduct High Holyday services in Philadelphia. One year when Rosh Hashanah began on a Sunday evening, our family drove down to Philadelphia a few days earlier, and that Saturday night Sherri and I met Carolyn and John for dinner at a favorite old country inn.

It was a pleasant reunion, as always. The talk centered on kids and careers, plans and dreams. And a brief discussion of John's health. He had undergone serious surgery, but despite some residual problems, the prognosis was hopeful.

We said good-bye in the parking lot. The men kissed the women. The women kissed each other. And John and I gave each other the kind of awkward hugs men who really care about each other engage in.

We walked to our separate cars. I watched John and Carolyn move away into the autumn drizzle.

Just before Thanksgiving Sherri spoke with Carolyn. After she hung up, I asked, as always, for the report on John. Carolyn had said that things were really going well. Almost too good to be true. Better than in a very long time. Plans for their family vacation to Hawaii were going full steam ahead.

But just hours after that telephone conversation John had a seizure, stopped breathing for too many minutes, and suffered severe brain damage. He spent several weeks in intensive care. Months at a rehabilitation hospital. When we visited him in early March, his only word was "Huh."

Then the final medical catastrophe: John died two weeks after our last visit.

What was helpful for me — what always seems to be helpful — was the opportunity I had to collect my thoughts and speak about John. I was honored to be able to deliver a eulogy for him. Five hundred people crowded into the Swarthmore Presbyterian Church to say good-bye. I had no idea that John had touched so many lives. The presence of that crowd was reaffirming.

What I mentioned that day was the surprise and reassurance I felt as I discovered the many ways I remembered John. Of course, our last hours with him were devastating. But given the charge to reflect on his life, a rush of happy, even mundane, memories quickly overcame the recent very sad ones, and those memories brought me comfort.

Cross-country skiing up at our home in Vermont. That's how I especially remembered John: ruddy face, purposeful strides. A vital, strong, engaging presence, loving what he was doing, breathing the heavy breath of an athlete, stopping to rest and admire the beauty of the countryside, the crispness of the day. And always with the twinkling eyes, the hearty laugh, the charming, almost impish smile across his face.

That's how I like to remember John. And in another way, too.

It was winter 1990. Our family had moved from Philadelphia to Vermont the previous summer, and early in December our new home was finally completed. The Walter family, our first guests, arrived just two weeks after we moved in.

We eagerly awaited them.

The big Buick wagon pulled into the garage, and after the hugs and kisses, John told us of their harrowing trip, which included a 360-degree spin-around on the icy New York Thruway. But, as I recall, John's intellect and fabulous, innate curiosity enabled him to analyze that experience, and ultimately to understand it as being, yes, frightening, but also interesting. To John, life was always interesting, and he could see what others so often missed.

We unloaded the car, then toured the house. John examined the posts and the beams, the drywalls and the electrical service. As always, John's was an opinion I valued much more than other people's. Because John was direct, without guile, an honest man fortified with the common sense and savvy of a country boy and refined with the sophistication of a lawyer and educator. He was a Renaissance man.

He pronounced the house wonderful. It felt like a blessing.

But what I think about most, and what continues to amaze me, is how even very simple events take on unexpected significance after a friend dies.

Can the thought of shoveling slush across a garage floor bring a lump to one's throat? Without question. That's what John and I found ourselves doing one afternoon. Just talking while pushing that slush out of the garage and onto the gravel driveway. Such an unimportant event. I recall it perfectly. And what I wouldn't give for the chance to do it with John again.

At other times I've wondered: Is there anyone who ever beat John to the dishwasher after a meal? I never had a chance. He would leap for the sink, and by the time everyone else moseyed over, John would already be scrubbing the plates.

Nobody has ever put cleaner plates into a dishwasher than John.

And the evenings. The four teenagers retired to the third floor with their nonsensical videos. The four parents sat by the fire and talked, mostly about the kids. We encouraged one another, exchanging those feelings of anxiety that parents of teenagers are naturally meant to feel.

Years ago a poet, victim of a terminal disease and anticipating his death, wrote a piece called "How Can I Not be Among You?" An apt title, expressing succinctly the mystery of death. "How can I not be among you?"

How can John Walter, with whom we ate dinner at one

holiday season — how can John not be among us? How is it that one year he was present? And the next year he was not.

There are no answers. Just questions. And feelings of vulnerability. And sadness. Of course. Sadness.

But what I do know is that I think of John. I think about him a lot, even as, at other times, I think about my father, my uncle, my grandparents.

I think about them on formal occasions, such as holiday memorial services when the liturgy, the music, and the silence prompt us to remember. But equally important, I think of them on so many varied occasions, times that I would expect and times that really surprise me.

I think of John often, speak about him often.

But it's strange: The most powerful memory of John comes to me when I'm in our garage. I'm usually there alone, and have time to reflect. And what I visualize every time, what I see in the holiness of memory, is that December afternoon when John and I casually grabbed two old snow shovels and together cleaned up the slush that had fallen from the cars. We pushed the gray ice and snow along the garage floor and outside into the winter sunlight.

A very ordinary activity. It has become a sacred moment that I will treasure forever.

The questions still flow. Why John Walter? Why did he need to suffer so, why did he die in his prime? No answers, of course. I wasn't expecting them.

But this I do know: There is a part of John — as there is a part of everyone we have loved — that can never completely pass away. There is something that can never wholly die as long as we remember them, as long as we keep them in our hearts through our private musings, our unexpected dreams, our conscious determination to allow them to bless our lives.

Mild winter afternoons. Shoveling slush out of a damp

garage. Those are the moments I sense John's presence most vividly.

I feel a sadness, of course. And John Walter's abiding absence.

But also gratitude for the healing power of everyday memories that surprise us, even cheer us, at the most unexpected times.

– II –

From Childhood to Maturity
and Youth to Age

5. Afghans

On a page in a photo album is a black-and-white picture of a little boy and a middle aged woman standing in a chicken coop placing eggs into a basket. The little boy, perhaps three or four years old, wears a coat and matching cap, and he looks into the camera with very wide eyes. Examining the old photograph, one might not be able to determine whether the look on the child's face was one of excitement, surprise, or fear.

I happen to know that it was indeed a look of fear, because I was that little boy, and I remember that time.

When the photograph was taken, I was frightened, because surrounding me were all of the chickens in the henhouse, and when you stand only three feet tall, a medium-sized chicken is a very big, frightening bird with sudden movements, a sharp beak, and ominous-looking pointed feet.

I also remember that the fear did not last very long. I overcame the initial fright and eventually discovered that collecting eggs was good fun. It was fun because the woman standing behind me in the picture — the woman who was bending over, encircling my small frame — was my grandmother. And after the picture was taken, she showed me, in her gentle way, that collecting eggs was a happy game.

I suppose that not too many American Jewish kids had grandparents who owned a chicken farm, but that's how and where I remember my father's parents. My grandfather died when I was quite young, and I can only recall being with him on a few occasions. One of those times was a big Passover seder at the farm. I can see exactly where he sat; I can even recall that he hid the *afikomen,* matzoh put aside for the children to find, in a magazine rack beside the brown recliner.

But I remember my grandmother very well.

She and I were always like soulmates, probably because we shared the same initials. Her name was Rae, Rachel Abelson Alper, and since my middle name is Abelson, we were both RAA. That might have been why I became closer to her than her other fifteen grandchildren. Maybe there were different reasons.

She had a beautiful face and a sweet voice, and she loved to sing songs in Yiddish and English. When I appeared in her kitchen, she'd often turn from the counter, hands covered in flour, and greet my arrival, singing, "If I knew you were comin', I'd have baked a cake. Baked a cake. Baked a cake. If I knew you were comin', I'd have baked a cake. Howdy do. Howdy do. Howdy do."

We had a special bond, Grandma and I. During the years of her widowhood she secretly saved her "house money" to help put me through college.

In 1958, just after my Bar Mitzvah, Grandma realized a lifelong dream and sailed to Israel aboard the *S.S. United States*. When she returned, she brought me a gift, a lovely little Passover Haggadah. Inside the front cover she wrote that she hoped I would enjoy the Haggadah as much as she enjoyed bringing it to me from Israel. Typical of Grandma, she spelled Israel I-S-R-E-A-L. I chuckle about that today, knowing that if she were here, she would laugh the loudest.

Rae Alper had her devilish side, too. She and my mother once took a short trip to Bermuda. As they returned through U.S. Customs, the officer asked their places of birth. "Baltimore," my mother responded. And Grandma confidently asserted, "Providence, Rhode Island."

As soon as they settled into the taxi, my mother, slightly bewildered, turned to Rae. "How could you say Providence? You were a baby when you came here, but you were born in Russia." "Of course," Grandma replied somewhat conspiratorially, "but if I told him that, he'd have arrested me!"

My grandmother died in 1972, leaving many memories and, even better, some precious physical reminders: a photo of us collecting eggs; a small Haggadah whose loving inscription still makes me laugh more than three decades later; and a big green afghan. Grandma knitted that afghan for me at the time of my birth, as she did for her first ten grandchildren. In the center, in large letters, is "our" monogram: RAA.

That afghan rested on the foot of my bed throughout my childhood. It was the "extra" blanket, not tucked in among the regular bedcovers but ready just in case. In the middle of the night, if I woke to feel a chill, I could simply reach down, pull up the afghan, and fall back into comfortable, protected sleep. It even went with me to college and seminary.

By the time Sherri and I married, the afghan had become quite tattered. Its green yarn had faded unevenly, and the corners had begun to unravel. Nothing lasts forever, and that afghan had seen many better days and nights. Besides, we had received lovely blankets as wedding gifts. The afghan found its way to a box in the storeroom.

Years later our son, Zack, attended overnight camp for the first time, spending four weeks at a wonderful place called Farm and Wilderness in the hills of Vermont. Vermont nights, even in midsummer, are often crisp, and the camp recommended a warm sleeping bag and an extra blanket, just in case. The old afghan was pressed into service once again.

Like all parents, we were concerned about our nine-year-old being away from home for the first time at overnight camp. But something in me, maybe a little bit of the mystic, figured that everything would be all right because, in a way, Grandma was taking care of her great-grandson whom she never knew. How she would have loved him! But I was certain that the work of her hands would keep him warm during cold mountain nights, just as the beauty of her life continues to keep me warm, and comfortable, and secure.

– ❖ –

My grandmother was an artistic knitter, and since I was the fifth grandchild for whom she made an afghan, the finished product was quite handsome. Effectively contrasting dark and light green; a variety of stitches, every one perfect, all part of an elegant, symmetrical design.

My friend Sheryl has an afghan, too. Turns out it's just about as old as mine, but quite a bit uglier. A cacophony of heavy yarns of wildly contrasting, sometimes clashing colors are woven into a huge rectangle with no distinct pattern holding it together. To be charitable, one might call it "interesting." Yet it lies on Sheryl's family room couch during all but the hottest months. Sheryl, her sister, and her kids use it frequently.

When I told my friend the story of my afghan, Sheryl told me the story of hers.

Sheryl's father, Monty Kligerman, played the violin as a child and was considered a prodigy. Music was his life, and the prestigious Juilliard School formed a part of his education as a young man. Later he earned his undergraduate degree and a masters in music from Columbia University. Without question, his teachers predicted, Monty would become a fine conductor, combining his unique musical talent with his willingness to work hard in pursuit of his dreams.

But when he was in his mid-twenties, World War II erupted, and Monty Kligerman joined the United States Army. The violin, the bow, the baton, would all need to wait. Monty's hands now held a rifle.

Monty rose to the rank of lieutenant, and one day, while on patrol with four of his men, their jeep was struck by German sniper fire. The vehicle turned over, trapping all the soldiers except Monty, who had been thrown clear. Despite grave danger, Monty risked his life to successfully rescue all of the badly wounded men. For his outstanding act of selfless bravery, Monty was awarded the Bronze Star.

While extricating his fellow soldiers, Monty, too, was wounded. A bullet passed through one of his arms. Another shattered his left hand.

Monty never played the violin again, never became a conductor, never pursued a career in music. He married, had two daughters, and made a modest living in several occupations: selling retail, designing kitchens, selling insurance, whatever. Music was no longer a part of his life. Even recordings and concerts became unimportant. Perhaps the memories of opportunities lost were simply too painful. He died at age sixty-seven.

During Monty's six months recovering in a hospital, one of his doctors suggested that he try to learn knitting in order to restore at least some functioning to his badly damaged hand. And that's just what he did. In a slow, agonizing way Monty Kligerman learned how to knit. Eventually he took up a real project, using whatever scraps of yarn he could find. When he finished, he had created that large, somewhat disproportional multicolored afghan. The one now in Sheryl's family room: a symbol of a life transformed, redirected by fate.

It's really quite amazing when you think about it: how a split second changes a life, how one split second has an impact on the lives of so many other people. Somewhere in Europe, in the heat of battle, a man abandoned his own security and exposed himself to grave danger while rescuing four fellow soldiers. In the process he was severely wounded, his life permanently changed.

For Monty Kligerman, what it meant was this: His music would never be heard. The shattered hand would never again hold a violin or a bow or a baton. The damaged fingers would attend to other, more mundane tasks. First, knitting, in order to regain some function. Then stocking shelves, measuring stoves and sinks, and punching numbers into an adding machine.

Another result of those German bullets whizzing through a forest in Europe, 1944: Thousands, perhaps even hundreds of thousands, of people would never enjoy the splendid artistry of this Juilliard-trained musician.

And yet, to the four men whom Monty rescued, that sacrifice meant nothing less than life for them, for their children, their grandchildren, and the generations that will follow.

$$- \diamond -$$

When we think about it, there are so many elements of the legacy people leave behind. Primarily life itself, in the form of children, and grandchildren, and great grandchildren. Or people to whom life was given in a different way, as when Monty Kligerman rescued his men from certain death.

And then there are the other pieces of a legacy. Inanimate objects. A photo, a watch, a favorite coffee cup. One woman I know hates all weapons and reminders of war, but cherishes a toy cannon made by her late father.

All of these objects are so precious as they help us to remember.

For Sheryl it's the afghan. That homely, bulky mélange of yarn that always awaits her on the family room couch. Sometimes she thinks about its meaning, its origin, but usually it's just there, to be grabbed and used late into chilly nights after the thermostat has cycled back to lower numbers. She snuggles into it, watching television or reading quietly. The drafts cannot penetrate it. The weight of it on her shoulders is comforting. Its size surrounding her makes her feel small. Protected. Embraced.

Just a nubbly old afghan. Ugly. Unpatterned.

Priceless.

Made by the hands of Monty Kligerman. Her father.

6. A Private Ceremony

"It's a swear word."

"Is not. It's the name of a kid who was in Miss Brady's class three years ago. His first name was Larry."

"Unh-uh. It's a swear." I was looking at a multisyllabic, vaguely medical sounding pencil scrawl inside the front cover of the used fifth-grade math text that Elinor Cato, the book monitor, had just placed on my desk.

"Ask Miss Brady. She'll tell you."

"*You* ask Miss Brady."

"Why should I? It's your book. You're just a chicken. Alper's a chicken."

At age ten I was no chicken. I was a fish who, at that moment, had taken my friend Ricky's bait. While other appointed officials — the inkwell monitor, the pencil monitor, the eraser monitor — fulfilled their opening-day assignments, I marched up to Miss Brady and asked her the meaning of the word I had found in my book.

She sent me to the principal.

Thus began the first of my two serious encounters with Miss Coleman.

As I recall, the CEO of John Howland Elementary School handled the situation rather gracefully, maintaining a very serious demeanor throughout and probably more amused at Miss Brady's discomfort than at some former fifth grader's attempts to win graffiti immortality. She silently read the word, asked if I knew the name of its author ("No, Miss Coleman. I just got the book this morning. But Ricky says he thinks it's somebody's last name."), and carefully removed every letter with a crumbly pink eraser. Then, for good measure, she turned a pencil on its side and with broad strokes coated those three square inches with graphite.

I returned to the classroom. By this time Ricky had alerted nearly everyone to his exploit. I pretended to ignore their grins, and at the first opportunity I subtly meandered over to the dictionary. The word was not listed. Too sophisticated for the children's Webster's supplied to us by the Providence, Rhode Island, Board of Public Education. It was only during recess out on the black-topped playground (the arena of real education) that I discovered the authentic meaning of the word.

It was definitely a swear word.

In hindsight I have to admire Miss Coleman. Our principal reacted with appropriate sternness but also fairly, without reprimanding me for what was, after all, a simple act of intellectual inquiry. I'm sure, though, that when she retired to the teachers' lounge later that morning, she doubled over with laughter, telling her colleagues, "You won't *believe* what word Bobby Alper found in his math book!"

John Howland was organized on the half-year system. First, kindergarten, then grade 1A and 1B, and on to 2A and 2B. I entered kindergarten in January, just before my fifth birthday, and expected to become a first grader the following January. But one day in the spring it was Maureen Blunt's turn to walk down the row of children and recite everybody's name. When she reached me, I was squatting down on one knee. At that moment our teacher, Miss Blake, uttered fateful words that shaped my life and determined much of my destiny: "Bobby is tying his shoe. Why, he's ready for the first grade!"

In September I entered 1A. I often wondered if, among many other results, being deprived of a semester of kindergarten had anything to do with my becoming a comedian thirty-six years later.

The half-year system provided us with double the number of elementary school rites of passage. In grade 5B I was appointed auditorium lights turner-on and turner-off, with the heady responsibility of pushing twelve white buttons (lights on) or twelve black buttons (lights off) in a room just off the stage. By grade 6A I had advanced to motion-picture projector operator. Not only did I get to watch lots of instructional movies with ponderous sound tracks, but, better, I could shout orders to the lights turner-on. With each half year came new jobs and new status.

Sixth grade found me at the very top of the pecking order, and I savored that coveted position. My sister took pleasure in taunting me, warning me that after the boys' gym classes at the junior high school everybody had to take showers and parade naked in front of everyone else — in alphabetical order. I wanted to stay at John Howland forever, or at least change my name to Wilson.

In September of that final year Miss Coleman invited a few of us to join the elite, the proud, the authoritarian: We became members of the Safety Patrol. This meant that when school let out, at noon and again at three-thirty, we would stand at the nearby intersection guarding the crosswalks with large flags. It also meant that we could wear white chest sashes and badges for the entire year, and travel to Washington, D.C., for the American Automobile Association Safety Patrol convention, where we continued the long-cherished John Howland School Safety Patrol tradition of tossing water balloons out of the windows of the Annapolis Hotel.

Our responsibilities were fairly routine. But one afternoon while I was on duty, a terrible thing happened. A car, moving very slowly, ran over a beautiful cocker-spaniel puppy that lived in the house across the street from the school. I actually saw the tire roll over the puppy's body, and stood frozen as the poor animal writhed and then lay silent with blood dripping from its mouth. I dashed into the main office and blurted out to the secretary, "Someone just ran over a dog!" The woman barely looked up from her typewriter, shrugged her shoulders, and murmured, "So?"

"Well," I continued, very agitated, "can you please call a veterinarian?"

"No."

I don't recall what happened after that. But her indifference appalled me then. Now, too.

Just a word, a sigh, a grimace, from her would have made all the difference.

There were about ten of us on the patrol, all boys and evenly divided between 6A and 6B. In 1956 raising and lowering a red flag with the word "Stop" written across it was considered work only a man could handle. In late January the 6B's would move on to Nathan Bishop Junior High School to face what I was convinced would be alphabetical showering, while those of us who remained advanced to the top leadership roles.

One day in the middle of January my teacher, Miss Toole, passed along a message. At the third bell I was to report to the principal's office. I wasn't nervous. After all, I was always a well-behaved kid, saving my troublemaking for Hebrew School. But as the minutes passed, I grew more and more curious, and a little excited.

The only personal encounter I ever had with Miss Coleman was during the math book graffiti episode. Otherwise, of course, I had watched her at assemblies and observed her when she came into our classroom for her "private-public talks" with our teacher.

"Miss Toole," she would say in a loud voice, looking at us and not at Miss Toole, "I understand the members of your class are working *very* hard on their reading projects."

"Yes they are, Miss Coleman," she would answer, also surveying the room. "And if the book reports are handed in on time and neatly done, I think we just might be able to schedule that trip to tour the Old Stone Bank." We would look at one another with excited but restrained expressions. After all, we had been eavesdropping.

The third bell rang at 11:05. Miss Toole handed me a hall pass and sent me off to what would be my second and final private encounter with Miss Coleman. I presented myself to the nasty secretary, who mumbled that I should go right into the principal's office, where I found Miss Coleman sitting at her desk, writing. She rose from her high-back leather chair, partially closed the door, and picked up a large manila envelope from a coffee table in front of the couch.

Our meeting lasted only a minute or two. "Bobby," she said, "as you know, Chesley and Larry will be going to Nathan Bishop in a few days. I have decided to appoint you lieutenant of the Safety Patrol. Charles Pfaffman will be the captain. Congratulations." I grinned broadly and thanked her as she reached into the envelope. My mind was doing cartwheels. I'm gonna be the lieutenant! Yahoo!

She carefully withdrew a thin object wrapped in tissue paper and placed it on the table. Next, she reached over and unclasped the all-silver AAA Safety Patrol badge I wore on my white sash, replacing it with a shiny new silver-and-red lieutenant's badge.

Miss Coleman, tall, proper, austere Miss Coleman in her dark business suit and no-nonsense glasses, took one step backward to admire me and my new badge. She clasped her hands together, raised her eyebrows, and smiled approvingly.

Then she bent down, awkwardly, even shyly, and kissed me on the cheek.

Her nod indicated that I could return to my class. I walked through the empty corridors, thrilled with my Safety

Patrol promotion and confused over the meaning of that kiss. It was so unlike Miss Coleman. So out of character. It certainly was not sexual, not child abuse; and as for me, I did not have a crush on Miss Coleman. In short order I decided that the kiss was, simply, nice. It made me feel extra special, secretly valued. I had been selected to witness a very different, affectionate side of our principal. It was an honor.

I often thought about Miss Coleman as I grew older, especially the brief kiss this formal, aloof, well-defended disciplinarian gave me on that January morning. It was no small thing: She took a risk, going out of character for those few seconds to reveal to me a sweet, hidden tenderness others never saw.

— ❖ —

On the top shelf of the armoire in my bedroom there's a small old wooden box with an elephant design on the lid and a flimsy little latch to keep it closed. Rattling around inside is my old collection of stuff: a rare Adlai Stevenson campaign pin, cuff links, "booster" buttons for my high school newspaper, some coins from Israel and Russia and Morocco.

And a silver-and-red badge proclaiming "American Automobile Association Safety Patrol. Lieutenant."

Miss Coleman gave me that badge, along with a kiss. Apparently, she liked me. That meant a lot to me back in the sixth grade.

It still does.

7. Shadowed Celebrations

Years ago I heard a story about an elderly woman who was dying of cancer.

Almost completely confined to her hospital bed, she grew weaker day by day. But her spirit was strong, endearing her to the medical staff. The woman had a goal: Her granddaughter was to be married, and she was absolutely determined to attend her wedding.

She was willing to do whatever was necessary to get there: took all her medicines, endured some pain, attempted to leave her bed whenever possible, just to fight off the debilitation of a progressing disease.

And she succeeded. On the day of the ceremony the nurses swarmed around her as if *she* were the bride. They dressed her, combed her hair, applied makeup, and sent her wheeling down the corridor accompanied by her children in their gowns and tuxedos. A festive sight. A melancholy sight, too.

That evening the woman returned to her hospital bed, exhausted, elated. Her favorite night nurse stopped by to offer congratulations, not only on the wedding, but on her having beaten death's timetable.

"You must be very happy tonight," the nurse offered. "You did it. You really did it!"

The woman, surprisingly, was not about to simply accept the good wishes. Rather, she looked up from her pillow, thought for a moment, and said, with the slightest glimmer in her eye, "Yes, I did. But you know: I have another granddaughter...."

– ❖ –

I must admit that often, when I officiate at life-cycle events, I intentionally put myself on automatic pilot. Just let me get through the ceremony, keeping it warm and aesthetically pleasing. I've discovered that it can be dangerous to think too much. Several times, as I watched fathers take leave of their daughters and hand them off to the new man in their lives, I began to picture myself in the same position with my own daughter. Then I became slightly tearful. The only antidote was to switch images quickly and focus on Mel Brooks.

So much goes on among families during life-cycle events. Triumphs. Reconciliations. A penultimate step toward dissolution. The opening of wounds. The healing of wounds. What I witness is just the tip of an iceberg, and besides, everyone is usually on their best behavior.

As for some people, when I learn their stories, I just wonder how they could get through the day at all.

I think especially of one Bar Mitzvah. The participants included Mom and Dad, the Bar Mitzvah boy, three grandparents, aunts, uncles, cousins, and lots of friends. The ceremony went off without a hitch. Later there were plenty of good, warm feelings all around as smiles and congratulations wafted through the modest reception. The adults chatted and the kids ate everything in sight, then ran through the synagogue with the boys becoming increasingly disheveled and the girls, taller and more sophisticated, looking appropriately disgusted.

Yet remembering that scene from the distance of the years, sort of hovering above it in my mind, I am aware that the event lacked a certain completeness.

The Bar Mitzvah boy had a sister, fifteen and a half at the time of her brother's religious achievement. She did not attend the ceremony in a new dress and womanly stockings and lipstick. Her name was not mentioned publicly, only whispered privately among the guests. At the moment her entire extended family gathered to celebrate her brother's Bar Mitzvah, she sat alone, forty miles distant, in a psychiatric hospital, halfway through a ten-month confinement.

Years later it occurred to me: How could that mother and father have made it through the day's festivities? How do people successfully mask heartbreak and participate in — even enjoy — a special event? For sanity's sake do we occasionally permit ourselves to repress thoughts of contemporary hell, or does a happy celebration itself somehow allow pain to be endured?

I think about these issues often, especially when I am aware of a family with sadness or tension festering just below the surface. How do people survive moments like these?

How did the mother and father of that Bar Mitzvah boy endure? How could they watch their son perform, how could they smile with pride and socialize with family and friends while their hearts were torn by a mournful, haunting incompleteness?

I never asked them, although I had many opportunities.

They were my parents.

8. Moments of Connection

"What'll it be, hon?"

"Ah, I think I'll have the usual: a tuna hoagie with mayonnaise, hot peppers, and no onions. And a Diet Coke. Small."

"Any oil on the hoagie?"

"No thanks. Just mayonnaise."

"And how about you?"

"I'll have exactly the same thing. Tuna hoagie, mayonnaise, hot peppers, no oil or onions, and a small Diet Coke."

A typical lunch hour in the neighborhood sandwich shop. He and I sat there opposite each other in the small wooden booth awaiting our food while dishes clattered, waitresses bustled about us, and orders were shouted through the small opening in the wall behind the counter.

Our conversation: the usual banter. Vacation plans, family matters. He told me a joke, but of course I had already heard it. A brief discussion of mutual acquaintances.

And then a reference to current events. The news that week was full of reflections on the bombings of Hiroshima and Nagasaki and accounts of the final days of World War II. It was only interesting history to me; I was too young to remember. But not my friend.

A flashback. His face darkened as he began to share a memory.

The small lunchroom seemed to lose its reality. As he began to talk, the sounds of silverware and the cash register and other patrons' conversations faded, then ceased. Our booth became a private confessional, and it was as though the two of us were completely alone while he spoke.

"I remember that day as clearly as if it were yesterday," he began. "I had been at school, and when I came home in the afternoon, I noticed that something was very different in our house. It was dark. All the lights were out. I knew something terrible had happened.

"My father was sitting on the couch in the living room just...sort of staring. No sounds. No words. He was holding a telegram in his hands: 'We regret to inform you that your son was killed in action on June 8, 1944, during the Allied invasion of Normandy, France.'

"Within a month," he concluded, "my father's hair turned completely white."

From out of another world two tuna hoagies arrived and were thrust onto the table between us. Our conversation drifted seamlessly into other areas, but I noticed that twice during the next few minutes my companion removed his glasses and rubbed his eyes, as if to soothe an irritation. From my close vantage point directly across the table I saw the tiny tears escape his glistening eyes just before his quick recovery.

The meal continued. Topics of conversation: the baseball season, the refreshingly mild humidity of the day, a new movie.

During the remainder of the meal — and during the days that followed — I thought about my reaction to my friend's brief story, my reaction to my friend's pain. I had been taken off guard. Should I have tried to be empathetic? Should I have encouraged his tears, should I have attempted to draw him out as a form of healthy catharsis?

Ultimately I decided that those minutes in the restaurant were, for my friend, distressing, but also, in their own way, healthy, and that no particular response was called for.

And I also realized that the encounter was, for me, a beautiful honor, one of those rare moments when, unexpectedly, one human being allows another to enter his life and explore with him the source of his pain as well as the ongoing, eternal strength of a relationship between brothers, a relationship that death could not erase.

An honor. To witness and understand how, many decades later, a man still actively grieves over his elder brother's death.

The phrase "time heals all wounds" is often misunderstood. An open sore, for example, may heal. The skin grows together, renewing itself and forming a barrier against infection. But that new skin, that healed skin, is always more tender than the surrounding area. More sensitive. More fragile. And each time the healed skin comes in contact with a foreign object, there is a reminder of the initial injury. The skin is healed. The tenderness remains.

The tenderness remains. What is it that provokes these flashbacks? Calendrical events, of course. Birthdays and anniversaries and the changing of the seasons. Sacred holidays and their memorial services when we join in community to recall our beloved departed and acknowledge our shared humanity.

But there are other moments that come upon us unexpectedly, brushing against that tender scar and reawakening memories thought dormant: the taste of food prepared or seasoned in a unique way; the sound of a certain expression or accent; a stranger's face that is startlingly familiar.

Even the smell of cigars.

I don't like cigars or the odor they leave. But my grandfather, whom I loved, smoked four or five a day. Whenever I enter a room in which there hangs the residue of cigars, I fully expect Grandpa Edgar to rise from his big easy chair to greet me.

The evocative embrace of memory. Sometimes painful, sometimes tantalizing. Echoes of the past return to us over and over again.

The wounds heal, but the tenderness remains. The years

pass and the hurt subsides, but it surely never vanishes completely...as long as love endures.

It feels good to remember. In the traditional settings of home and worship. And in the most unexpected places: a room reeking of stale cigars.

Or in a crowded lunchroom on a midsummer day, over tuna hoagies with mayonnaise, hot peppers, no oil or onions.

– III –

From Innocence
to Awareness and Ignorance
to Knowing

9. The Blink of an Eye

An overcast June afternoon. The soccer field bustled with activity. The band warmed up, the graduates lined up, and the headmaster tried to keep his chin up as he worried over whether he should have moved the event into the gymnasium.

Commencement day for the Burr and Burton Seminary of Manchester, Vermont.

A strange name for a high school. It started out as an academy to train Congregationalist ministers, then became a private high school with no religious affiliation. Manchester and the surrounding towns, including ours, send their kids to Burr and Burton, which occupies a dignified old gray stone building atop Seminary Avenue and several other buildings lining the north side of the hill.

Back at the turn of the century Seminary Avenue was just a dirt road. A collection of memoirs by local residents relates how, on many evenings around dusk, two little girls, one who lived in a big white house and the other, her cousin from Rensselaer, New York, would scamper onto the street and dig holes.

Not large pits, just distractions; just large enough so that the horses and wagons carrying visitors would have to slow up and go around the depressions or risk an uncomfortable bump or two.

These were the moments the girls eagerly awaited. They would hide in the bushes, and as soon as the tourists' carriages slowed, they'd race out taunting, "City pups! City pups!" Then they'd run back, giggling, to the safety of the bushes.

It was great fun on a summer evening.

The little girls grew up. The one who lived in the big white house was one of the first young women to graduate from the high school at the top of her hill. She remained in that house, though; lived there almost to the very end of her long life.

Decades passed. Some things changed, some did not. Seminary Avenue was paved. White marble sidewalks that sparkled in the sun now lined its borders. But the tourists kept coming. People kept visiting the village, marveling at its dignified beauty, its gentle pace.

One summer evening a young family ambled down Seminary Avenue. They had rented a home in the village for their vacation. It was one of those perfect strolls. The father and mother walked together and talked quietly. The boy, eight years old, darted off from side to side, carefully searching for additions to his smooth rock collection.

The little girl, four and a half, had recently learned how to skip. The marble sidewalks provided her with a special challenge. Tentatively, then with more and more confidence, she bounded ahead at a distance that pulled taut the line between independence and security.

As the family neared the bottom of Seminary Avenue, the mother noticed the old woman standing on her porch, reaching down, trying to retrieve something. A coupon of some sort, a piece of paper that had fluttered out of the newspaper she had been reading.

The mother mounted the steps, caught the coupon, and handed it to the woman. Over the next few minutes, during a brief conversation, the woman explained how she had lived in that very house for eighty-four of her eighty-nine years. She knew everybody — she knew *about* everybody — in the village.

But before any words were exchanged, before introductions were made, the woman looked for a long moment at the beautiful little girl with light hair and sparkling eyes zigzagging her way down the marble sidewalks.

This night she didn't tease the tourists. This time she didn't giggle, then holler, "City pups! City pups!" Instead she gave a quiet sigh, looked off into the mountains, and said, "I used to skip like that."

It was almost as if she wanted her visitors to know that somewhere within her ancient, worn body there still existed a little girl...somewhere, deep in her memory, there still lived a happy, carefree child, now imprisoned by the years.

The mother and father realized during that poignant encounter, perhaps as never before or again, how swiftly time passes, and how precious is every moment of life.

The years moved on. Still loved and respected by the townspeople, the old woman finally entered a nursing home, and later, well into her nineties, she died.

As for the little girl who skipped down the marble sidewalks — the pretty little "city pup" with light hair and sparkling eyes — her family eventually moved to Vermont. And one cloudy June afternoon they watched her as she sat in the first row of Burr and Burton's graduating class.

My daughter.

Time passes quickly. So quickly. In the blink of an eye a mischievous little child who yelled "City pups" at tourists in horse-drawn wagons becomes an old woman, able only to dream of the time she used to skip down the street.

In the blink of an eye another little girl who just yesterday skipped down the marble sidewalks now sits with her classmates, ready to receive her diploma and soon head off to college.

I observed the ceremonies feeling as if I were two separate people: a father proudly watching his daughter complete a stage in her life and a kid myself, somehow dressed in middle-aged clothing and gray hair, wondering how I got here so fast and where the years have gone.

I recalled a time when I was fresh out of graduate school,

walking through a hotel lobby. I looked into the ballroom and saw a high school twenty-fifth reunion in progress. And the people were dancing. Dancing! I remember thinking. People *that* old and still dancing!

My own thirtieth high school reunion has come and gone.

That June afternoon the clouds threatened, the skies darkened and then lightened again, but it seemed as if the surrounding mountains, protective as always, held off the storm until well after the conclusion of the ceremonies. Now it was time to go home and prepare for the graduation party.

Arms full of gifts and robe and diploma, we walked down Seminary Avenue to the car. By coincidence, it was parked in front of that white house where the old woman had lived, the white house at which we'd paused to chat while our little children skipped and played on the marble sidewalk years ago.

During the first ten years of my rabbinate, it seemed as though every bride and groom chose "Sunrise, Sunset" from *Fiddler of the Roof* as their wedding march. I confess I became not only tired of the music, but cynical at the syrupy emotions of the lyrics. Puh-leeze, I would think. Give me a break with the "Is this the little girl I carried?" sentimentality.

It was sometimes just a bit too much, watching as the teary bride and more teary parents processed toward me, arm in arm.

But then, as I looked at the white house on Seminary Avenue and visualized a four-and-a-half-year-old skipping down the marble sidewalks, it was, of all things, the *Fiddler* lyrics that I reluctantly allowed to invade my brain: "Sunrise, sunset. Swiftly flow the years."

I used to grimace when I heard those words.

Not anymore.

10. I'd Give Anything . . . Anything

Westwood will shine tonight, Westwood will shine.
Westwood will shine tonight, Westwood will shine.
Westwood will shine tonight, Westwood will shine.
When the sun goes down and the moon comes up,
Westwood will shine!

It's a silly old camp song. Not much meaning to it either: After all, how can a camp "shine"?

Yet these words have been belted out over and over again through the decades by thousands of kids and their counselors, sung with fervor, gusto, even passion. Visions of guitar-playing songleaders whipping a campfire into a frenzy, or partisans at an intercamp sporting event screaming the Westwood mantra in an attempt to drown out the competition's supporters.

But "Westwood Will Shine" has never been sung with more zest, and love, than one July evening over a dinner table in Manchester, Vermont. Three onlookers watched in muted astonishment as a minister in his fifties and a rabbi fifteen years his junior joyously crooned the trite chorus to which there are no verses.

My initial encounter with Jerry took place on a Sunday morning at his Congregational church. Our family was vacationing in Manchester for the first time. I decided to take an interreligious busman's holiday and attend services.

Jerry's warm and appealing pulpit style was confirmed later, over coffee at the reception. I seem to recall that when I introduced myself as a vacationing rabbi from Philadelphia, Jerry replied that he, too, once served a congregation in Philadelphia, and that his favorite view of the City of Brotherly Love was the one he saw in his car's rearview mirror.

We exchanged letters. I must have written something about the tranquillity I had discovered in Manchester, because Jerry answered, "I am glad that you . . . and evidently thousands of others . . . think that all is calmness and peace in this little village. Someday I will acquaint you with the facts of life. It's really just another Peyton Place!"

And as to his gracious white village church with its tall spire amid the magnificent surrounding mountains, Jerry quoted a university professor who had been commissioned to write a history of the congregation in its 200th year: "I have a sense of marvel at the way the church and the town seem constantly oscillating between a sort of dignified serenity and complete bedlam."

Jerry and I enjoyed each other's company and eagerly looked forward to my increasingly frequent visits to Vermont. But it wasn't till a few years into our friendship that we discovered an unexpected bond linking us together.

Both Jerry and I had spent youthful summers at a place called Camp Westwood.

We weren't there at the same time. Jerry was a counselor and unit head during the late 1940s, and I began my tenure as a young camper only in 1953. Yet once we stumbled upon our common history during an intimate summer dinner party, the Westwood trivia began to flow as fast as the suddenly celebratory wine.

What was the name of the dining hall? The Merrimichi!

What stood behind the archery range? A nineteenth-century cemetery.

And why did all the campers envy the Catholic kids? They got to ride in a truck to mass every Sunday while the Jewish and Protestant kids had to stay behind in camp.

What was the slogan over the fireplace? "He who chops his own wood warms himself twice."

And the name of the troll who lived under the dock? Old Ned.

And so on throughout the meal. Stories, tales, trivia, memories. And songs. Jerry and I had a perfectly delightful evening.

Our dinner companions were patient. Tolerant. Bored.

What kind of camp was it that spawned a minister and a rabbi and, I imagine, some priests as well? Westwood was, and still is, a camp operated by the YMCA of Pawtucket, Rhode Island, the city next door to Providence, my hometown. In my first year at Westwood there were probably six Jewish kids in the whole place, it cost eighteen dollars a week, and it was an all-boys camp. By my sixth and final year the camp had turned coed, and the Jewish population had expanded as well.

I have a very vivid memory of the so-called nondenominational Sunday morning services we were required to attend in the rustic outdoor chapel by the lake. I can still visualize what had ultimately become an almost all-Jewish choir under the direction of Ellie Borenstein singing the hymn, "There's a Little Brown Church in the Vale."

Memories. Funny memories. Happy times. But there were some painful times as well.

Jerry and I talked about these, too, exchanging tales of the lonely, scary moments, especially my homesickness being away from my family for the first time as a child. And we shared stories of the growth and understanding that were part of the emergence into manhood marking Jerry's tenure at Camp Westwood.

There is one particular story Jerry told that has remained with me all these years.

"I never was an athlete," he began. "I don't think I ever

owned a baseball glove, and if someone threw a ball at me, I did the same thing as a kid that I do now. Either I wrap my hands around my head to protect my face or I stretch out my arms in front of me to try to knock the thing out of the air."

Jerry continued, "Oh, I would have loved to have been an athlete. Not even a real athlete. Just to be able to catch a baseball once in a while, or throw a football without looking like an off-balance ballerina. Tennis, badminton, volleyball. I was a flop. About the only sport I could handle fairly well was slow rowing.

"When the teams were picked, the way they used to do it in the old days, I wanted to dig a hole and dive in headfirst. They picked from the crowd: first, second, third, fourth choice, and so on down the line. And then inevitably, at the very end, one of the captains would bargain: 'Okay, I'll take Jerry this time, but that means I get first pick next time.' What humiliation!

"To make matters worse," Jerry continued, "my counterpart at Westwood, the other unit head, was a superathlete. Not only that, Jim was somewhat of a war hero, having served as a bombardier in Europe. Lean, muscular, and handsome, this guy could run and jump and bat and catch and swim and dive and wrestle better than anyone. An all-around jock. Mr. Macho. God, how I hated him. At least, I hated him at first. I had every reason to. He was a superman and there was I, a nonveteran seminary student, a nice person, mind you, but think of how I looked by comparison."

Jerry explained, "I hated him at first, but then something happened to change all that. An experience I will always cherish. It was a moment when I learned something profound about myself and about life.

"It was in the evening, after the campers had gone to bed;

and as I often did for relaxation, I walked into the dining hall, sat down at the old upright piano, and began to play. I wasn't a concert pianist. Just what you might call recreational tickling of the ivories. Not terrific. But not that bad, either.

"I never bothered to turn on the lights. The moon's reflection coming in off the lake provided enough illumination, and the low light was soothing.

"I enjoyed the contrast. During the day the dining hall was always bursting with the sound of chairs and tables scraping, dishes and silverware clanging, all competing with shouts and laughter and songs and cheers. Sometimes it was so loud that it's a wonder the roof could remain on the building.

"But at night, at night after the kids were in bed, when most of the staff would gather in the counselor's lounge next to the crafts barn, I would sit in the deserted dining hall at that piano playing from memory, composing a little bit here and there.

"And during the pauses between songs, even during the rests between measures, I could often hear the soothing sound of the small waves lapping at the shore of the lake or the steady clank of rowboats hitting against each other or against the dock. An occasional shout from one of the cabins in the distance; sometimes the melody of a campfire song floating across the lake.

"One night, in the midst of my playing, something seemed different, something unusual. I sensed a presence in the dining hall. I stopped my song in midmeasure, looked down the long row of tables, and realized that I was not alone. I squinted in the half-light, then realized that my fellow unit head, the war hero, the superathlete, was sitting next to the doorway at the far end of the room. Apparently he had been there for a long time, listening to me play. Perhaps he had sat there on other nights as well.

"The echo of my last notes faded, and then the only sounds were the little waves, the rowboats, other summer-night noises. I looked at Jim and gave him a nod of acknowledgment. And he sort of lowered his eyes and whispered, almost with embarrassment, 'I'd give anything — I'd give *anything* — to be able to play the piano like you do.'"

That was the end of the story. Decades later, Jerry still remembered. And why not? The magical encounter in the dim light of a summer camp dining hall literally changed the way he perceived the world, the way he perceived other people, and the way he perceived himself.

11. December Memories

My father used to take showers with the lady next door.

It was all pretty kosher. We rented half of a "duplex" house at 89 University Avenue in Providence, and the Winn family occupied the other half. "Duplex" means different things in various places; in Providence, a "duplex" was a house with two separate entrances and two mirror-image units. Ours had three floors and a basement suitable for Cub Scout den meetings.

The way the house was designed, the bathrooms on the second floor shared a common wall, tub alongside tub, and toilets back to back. The insulation was fairly thick, but subdued sounds could get through, and soon after the Winn family moved into 91 University Avenue, my father and Ruth Winn discovered that they observed similar morning shower routines. The muffled knocking back and forth on the tiles at 7:15 A.M., then a cute neighborhood joke, is now a piece of family folklore.

My mother and Ruth became friends immediately; forty years later and four hundred miles apart, they still dearly love each another. Shared laughter is what started it all off, but it was a hurricane called Carol that really brought us all together.

For eight days Providence was without electricity, and neighbors drew closer to one another. Cold food went into the Keoughs' old gas refrigerator at 85 University Avenue, while our battery-operated radio was the source for news and entertainment. The Winns' vast quantities of sporting equipment helped everyone pass the time until that late afternoon, when we were sitting on our porches and my mother suddenly yelled, "The lights are on!" Everyone rushed inside.

The bonding held.

The Winns' oldest son, Cooper David Winn IV, and I were classmates, though never best friends. Still, we spent lots of time together, as neighboring kids do, and some of the most memorable moments occurred around the December holidays. Chanukah at my house. Christmas at his house.

Mutual envy.

For me, Chanukah generally meant one gift from my parents per night, but factoring in additions from grandparents, other relatives, and friends, I averaged sixteen to twenty each season. Not bad. I would even feel a bit on the smug side as I walked to school in the morning reporting to Cooper on the prior night's take.

That is, I felt smug until early Christmas morning when I would race over to the Winns' side of the house to inspect the mountains of presents, the massive quantities strewn about the living room, such a volume of stuff that even the recognition in later years that the haul included a suspiciously large amount of underwear and socks could not make me rationalize away my jealousy.

The feeling of Chanukah has remained with me: our old tin menorah and the look, the smell, the soft, smooth texture of its candles, sometimes dripping their orange wax across my fingers. There were the traditional songs, the latkes and applesauce, and our one decoration, "Happy Chanukah," printed on colorful paper dreidels and placed across the dining room entryway. The sign was worn, faded, but it was our tradition, and for eight days it transformed the room into a chamber of happy expectation.

Most of my presents were modest. I loved to make Revell models of antique cars, and so something like a Stanley Steamer one night might be followed by a Stutz Bearcat the next. Another year it was accessories for my small American Flyer train set: One night it might be a new caboose, and another night a little building to place near the tracks. I remember categories of gifts, but the particulars have long faded.

Except for two presents that I've never forgotten.

The first was a twenty-six-inch English bicycle. It arrived in the year when I went for the gold in the "eight small presents or one big present" option game. Friday was the designated night, and as soon as the candles were lighted and the songs sung, I dutifully complied with the "Close your eyes tight" directive. The waiting seemed to go on forever as I listened to my father's grunts and a bumping noise coming up the cellar steps. When he approached the dining room, I heard the rhythmic, metallic sound of a spinning tire, and knew that my yearlong series of unsubtle hints had been acknowledged.

Later we went to synagogue, and before the service began, I stood in the foyer for what seemed like hours, watching as every person entered, brushing the snow off their coats and stomping their boots. I scanned the arrivals, looking for Joey or Sammy or Ricky or anyone else I knew. "Guess what! I got an English bike!"

Other Chanukahs, though, were not as festive. My parents constantly struggled financially, one of the consequences of my father's checkered career and made worse, later, by the albatross of medical bills from my sister's long illness.

My father was always involved in the paper business. During the eight years when we lived on University Avenue, he worked for at least six different companies in waste paper, paper chemicals, and wholesale tissue. Each position would begin with optimism and end with him returning home one night carrying his electric typewriter.

But he always bounced back, always landed another job somewhere, somehow. Yet the process was draining, and the weeks or months between paychecks grim. One of those dark periods coincided with Chanukah.

I knew things were tough that season. We didn't starve, but everything had to be cut back as we tried to make do on the salary my mother earned fitting women into corsets at the Peerless Department Store. "I know it's hard," she would say, "but some day our ship will come in." I believed her. Sometimes I could even visualize "our ship," a small speck on the horizon heading slowly, surely right for us.

"Our ship," burdened with riches, was still far out to sea when Chanukah began. This year, I knew, would not be like other years. The grandparents and a few of my parents' friends came through, but, my parents explained, I would need to understand that they simply couldn't afford presents this time. *Just this year. Next year will be better.*

Chanukah overlapped Christmas, fortuitously. The Winns were busy with their preparations, so I didn't see much of Cooper. I was glad school was already on vacation; there was no need to report to friends on my Jewish version of an empty stocking.

That Christmas morning I didn't rush next door.

On the final night of Chanukah my parents surprised me with a gift. It was a small one, they warned. Nothing very special. But I'd been so understanding of what was happening that they wanted me to have it. I felt a slight twinge of guilt over their sacrifice as I accepted the little package.

Inside the box was a plastic model for my collection, a replica of a Chris Craft cabin cruiser. Probably cost about $2.95. I glued it together the next day, and for years, until I went off to college, the little boat sat on a shelf in my bedroom. It was far from being my fanciest model. Though it's been long discarded, the thought of it means more to me now than it ever did back then.

When I look back on all those Decembers of my childhood, those often wonderful days of mystery, anticipation, celebration, I know for a fact that I received many dozens of presents over the course of the years. They form an indistinct blur. After all, a long time has passed.

In truth, of all those gifts, I can actually remember only two. Only two. One was a twenty-six-inch English bicycle. Shiny black, three-speed, with a headlight powered by a generator that spun alongside the tire and its own silver air pump latched to the frame.

The other was a plastic model boat.

12. Lust and Love

It's a good thing sensitivity training and sexual-harassment awareness weren't around in 1954, because I would have been in BIG trouble.

It was just before lunch, in Miss Hanley's fourth-grade class. I can't recall all of the details, but I do know that for some reason I snuck up beside Lenore Dubinsky, the prettiest girl in the class, and kissed her full on her right cheek. The recipient wrinkled her freckled nose, shot me a semidisgusted look, and continued her conversation with Tena Marks.

I retreated victoriously to my seat (front left side of the room, as always; my last name begins with "A"). And then my lips began to burn.

Not an intense heat. Just a kind of warm, tingly sensation. I didn't quite know what to make of it until I started thinking of the lyrics of a popular song, and the term "kiss of fire" began running through my mind. That's what it was! The kiss of fire! My nine-year-old mind convinced me Lenore was THE one, and that even though she completely ignored me now, we were somehow destined to be with each other. I needed only to wait for it to happen.

And so I waited. I never told Lenore about the kiss of fire. And I never dated her, although we were classmates right on through high school. Finally, though, it occurred to me that on the fateful day of the kiss, Lenore had probably applied some kind of medicine to her prepubescent face, and my sensitive, moist little lips initiated a chemical reaction that resulted in physical, but not really metaphysical, heat.

Ever since I began riding my battered little red Schwinn bicycle to Jeanne Brown's house in the second grade, or stood up Cory Goldenberg, my first real "date" in the third grade (it was a misunderstanding, and the following week

I took her to see *Hondo* in 3D), I always wrestled with the questions of love and marriage. Frequently I'd consider the fact that somewhere in the world there was a person I would marry. I probably hadn't met her yet. On the other hand, maybe I knew her well. Maybe it was even Lenore, or Cory, or Tena. It was fun to speculate.

It was also confusing. What exactly is love, and why do people choose each other?

When we think of it, we're all amateurs at selecting a marriage partner, unless, of course, we're approaching it for a second or third or fourth time, in which case our status lies somewhere between expert and serial failure. No matter how we go about it, though, it seems to me that one of the biggest stumbling blocks is the widely accepted and bizarrely inaccurate cliché, "It was love at first sight."

Really. How can one fall in love, true love, just by taking a look at a person? That's not love at all. It's lust.

I'm not frightened by the word *lust*. It's a good word, an apt word that describes what can be a very appropriate emotion in the right context. Lust is what draws people to each other, assuring the perpetuation of our species. One sees an attractive person "across a crowded room" and it can be "lust at first sight." Later, the lust might actually turn to love. And it might not.

Take, for instance, an average young lawyer, a fairly intelligent fellow cruising the Saturday night bar scene at a local restaurant. From out of the corner of his eye he spots an adorable young woman, nicely dressed, with an appealing figure and a pleasant manner. This could be love at first sight, he thinks, as he elbows his way through the raucous crowd.

And just as he closes in on this woman of his dreams, he hears her declare to those in her group, "Durn, don't that Rush Limbaugh just hit the nail on the haid?"

Our attorney may still feel a smidgen of lust, but love will probably not be an option here.

Just how does one make the transition from lust to love? Each person's stories are unique. Mine might be instructive.

One of the many times I fell in lust occurred during the early summer of 1964. I had finished my sophomore year at Lehigh University and was visiting my parents in Bennington, Vermont, the town to which they had moved after I graduated from high school. During earlier school vacations I had made some local friends, and that night I decided to visit Bill and his younger sister Alison at their home.

There wasn't a lot to do in Bennington, Vermont, in those days. Mainly what we'd do was watch a little television, walk outside and sit on someone's motorcycle, then go back for more TV. That was about it.

Except that on this particular night Alison was hosting a party for six or seven of her girlfriends with whom she had just graduated from high school. They were all sitting on the kitchen floor for some reason when I arrived, and from my vantage point, standing by the stove, I was able to survey the entire group to see if any interested me.

One did. I fell, slightly, preliminarily, in lust.

We dated a few times that summer, and then it was an on-again, mostly off-again relationship for the next six months. In February of my junior year I visited her in Manhattan. Then a freshman at Bennington College, she was spending her "nonresident term" interning at an accounting firm. We enjoyed a mildly beatnik evening, as was the custom of Bennington women and the men who squired them in that era. She wore black from head to toe. Our wanderings took us from an avant garde theater to a coffeehouse, all, of course, in Greenwich Village.

It was a delicious night, made even better when she agreed to attend a major party at Lehigh two weeks later.

The following Sunday evening I was summoned to the phone at the fraternity house. She was calling to back out. "I just got pinned."

Sure. Pinned. The old "engaged to become engaged" bit. I knew that "getting pinned" was something a Bennington woman wouldn't be caught dead doing. But maybe going to a fraternity party fell into that same category. Whatever the reason, I had been dumped.

Fast forward to late January of my senior year, when I had a few days to kill between semesters and now, finally, also had my very first car. Maybe she was back in New York, maybe even un-pinned. "And besides," I rationalized, "nearly a year has passed, so I'm ready to be humiliated again."

I tracked her down.

During this "nonresident term" she was not in Manhattan but, of all places, Scranton, Pennsylvania, the city to which her parents had recently moved. She was even happy to hear from me, although I suspect that, living temporarily in Scranton, she would have been happy to hear from anybody. A few days later I drove up to see her.

It's funny what you remember about events so long ago. My Rambler's transmission made strange noises on the drive up, and one repairman in Scranton warned that only a major overhaul would get me on the road again. Another mechanic tightened a plug, added some fluid, and the car was good for another six months until I sold it.

Most of all, of course, I remember my date. I guess that after the eighteen months of knowing her, I was still in lust. And proper lust does serve an important function — such as drawing me to Scranton in pursuit of a girl who had already rejected me several times. We decided to go to a good restaurant, one fancy enough to take reservations. This was

1966; I wore a suit and tie, and she wore her best dress. Black, of course.

That winter she was working as an aide at a school for severely retarded children, a sad place populated with about forty boys and girls, from infants to adolescents. On the way to the restaurant she suggested we detour slightly and stop by the school so she could show it to me.

It was more than thirty years ago, but I'll never forget what happened when we came through the large doors and into the foyer. Some of the staff and a few of the children were standing about or sitting on the floor of the adjacent rooms. As soon as we walked within their sight, we heard a very happy yelp as a five-year-old boy with Down syndrome raced awkwardly out of the living room and toward my date.

He was not a pretty sight. His shirt bore the remains of his recently eaten spaghetti dinner, and his cheeks were red with tomato sauce. A combination of old and new mucus, some dried, some still glistening, cascaded from his nose, and even an expert chemist would be incapable of determining all that was stuck to his hands.

I flinched as he drew closer, and prepared somehow to guard my newly dry-cleaned suit from what I knew would be a very grimy touch.

He ran toward us, calling out a word over and over, a word I could not understand. My date interpreted for me: It was her name that he was shouting with such delight.

Just as the little boy reached us, the Bennington girl in her black tights and best dress and long dangly earrings bent forward and with a graceful rhythm caught the child and lifted him in her arms till they were face-to-face, giving him the monumental hug he so correctly expected.

I looked on, amazed. I realized that in her schedule of priorities, her clothing and her combed hair and her freshly scrubbed face meant absolutely nothing in comparison to hugging that little boy.

I also realized that ever since I crashed a party eighteen months before, I had been in lust.

Now I was in love.

Three-and-one-half years later we were married.

– IV –

From Foolishness
to Discretion and Then,
Perhaps, to Wisdom

13. The Toll

Mr. Makeit.

Really. That was his name. As in "make it."

He was the John Howland Elementary School's physical-education instructor. Only back in the early fifties he was referred to as "the gym teacher." And with a name like "Mr. Makeit," one can only imagine the inventive ways we scatologically inclined fourth graders referred to him.

Mr. Makeit provided me with my first exposure to macho behavior. A couple of times each week my classmates and I would file to the basement, the girls heading down one stairway and the boys another. No lockers or gym uniforms or showers. Not even sneakers. Just a variety of physical activities in our street clothes and brown leather shoes. Still, the girls and boys were separated by a floor-to-ceiling divider that allowed nary a peek. To this day I have no idea what they did on the other side of that forbidding wall.

But I remember Mr. Makeit's class. He would have us run around the gym a few times, then line us up in four or five orderly rows. A short, stocky man with the requisite crew cut, always dressed in dark pants, a white short-sleeve shirt, and blue bow tie, he would stand front and center and wait for the chatter and the panting to die down. It didn't take long. Mr. Makeit played us like a symphony orchestra. We knew that as soon as we were quiet, he'd announce the day's activity.

If we were really good, really cooperative, if we lined up with all the military precision nine-year-olds can muster, Mr. Makeit would very deliberately sweep his eyes back and forth across the expectant faces, then glance upward in a contemplative, wrinkled-forehead stare. Ever so slowly, ever so dramatically, he would announce, "Today (pause) we're gonna play a game (pause) called (long pause) Scatter (pause) Dodge."

Pandemonium. Whoops and hollers and screams. We would have done "high fives," but we were a generation premature. Mr. Makeit took it all in, reveled in it. No doubt one of the highlights of his life.

Twenty seconds of celebration and then our hero's hand rose. Dead silence. Captains were appointed, teams selected, and a shriek of the whistle signaled the start of yet another game of Scatter Dodge.

I hated it.

First of all, I wasn't particularly delighted at always being one of the last chosen. But since there were a few even more awkward than I, at least I had a couple of opportunities to murmur to the boy next to me, "Oh, great. We got Philip."

Mainly, though, I just never could understand the thrill of throwing a large rubber ball at another person in an attempt to hit him and knock him out of the game. Of course, I didn't experience that particular "thrill" too often since, as a slow-moving target, I was frequently eliminated from the contest early on. A well-thrown ball would hit me in the corduroys. I'd give the expected grimace, then go sit on the bench with the other early losers and cheer for the remaining members of my team. Not that I cared. It's just what we knew we had to do.

I suppose the lofty purpose of Scatter Dodge was to teach coordination, teamwork, and macho behavior. It's a tough world, Mr. Makeit figured, and his job was to prepare us for what lay ahead. The lesson never quite worked for me, since even back then I would watch eager, aggressive classmates whomp each other and think, *this is really dumb.*

I never became a fighter. I avoided situations that could lead to trouble, and deftly talked my way out of a couple of potentially hazardous encounters with boozy fraternity brothers.

But there was one time when I nearly did become involved in an "act of aggression," as they say, an altercation with a pugnacious stranger.

As these things often do, it began with a confrontation by automobile.

I was meandering through an industrial park one afternoon, not paying particularly close attention to my driving since the road was straight and traffic was light. But I was jolted from my near-daydream when I almost plowed into a car that had stopped in the middle of the road without any apparent reason. No light. No intersection, driveway, or crosswalk. The fellow had just decided to pause for a moment, perhaps to read directions or look up a number for his mobile telephone.

It wasn't even a near-miss. I had time to apply my brakes and slow to a safe stop. But I was annoyed. If I were a more confrontational type, I would have exited my car and addressed the fellow as follows: "Sir. Stopping your vehicle for no apparent reason in the middle of a heavily traveled roadway forces fellow drivers to take unanticipated defensive maneuvers that could result in an accident with damage to the vehicles and injury to the driver and/or its occupants."

I could have said that. Instead, I honked the horn.

To me, it was just a friendly "Hey, let's get going here" kind of toot. Apparently the listener took it differently. Maybe he was in the midst of a bad day.

In any event, the other driver raced off ahead of me, but soon after he rounded a turn, he pulled off to the side of the road, jumped from the car, and as I drew near, angrily gestured for me to park my car behind his. Scatter Dodge and Mr. Makeit notwithstanding, I decided to decline the invitation. Instead, I passed by, smiled and waved pleasantly.

Now he was behind me. I could see his tight, menacing face in my rearview mirror, sometimes distant, sometimes close, as the speed and traffic dictated. We both drove up the wide ramp to the turnpike, and I figured I had seen the last of him when he chose a different ticket booth. I hoped he would head east; I was going west.

I relaxed into the rhythms of the highway, checking the rearview mirror and merging farther and farther left into the passing lane, which I favored. I'd nearly forgotten the encounter when suddenly there he was again, this time in the slower lane. I glanced over to the right for just a split second as my car drew up next to his. Apparently our earlier meeting was still churning in his mind. He greeted me through the device of a well-known digital signal. And a snarl. I sped on by.

Well, I thought, at least I'm finally rid of this character. He didn't seem to be following me. And besides, it's a big, long turnpike. A few minutes later I reached my exit and began to ascend the winding ramp that would take me off to the side, then over the roadway and up to the row of collectors. Eight lanes. I chose the shortest line. Guess who pulled in behind me.

Cautiously, with an unobtrusive elbow on the doorsill, I locked the car, all the time shifting my eyes to the rearview mirror. He sat there, glaring at me, agitated but not making any move to get out of his car.

Four cars idled ahead of me. Then three, then two. I contemplated my options. I knew I had a chance to do something unique. I realized the opportunity that was mine at this moment.

One car left and now I rolled up to the collector. I took a

final look at the grim face in the rearview mirror, and then I did it.

I paid his toll.

Traffic was heavy on the four-lane freeway I entered, but I noticed the guy's car behind me in the distance. I zipped ahead in the passing lane, and could see him weaving in and out of both lanes in a safe but determined effort to catch up with me. It took about five miles of deft maneuvering, but finally he pulled up on my right, both of us clipping along at a steady sixty-five.

He bowed his head slightly and tapped the side of his eyebrow in an informal, grateful salute. An acknowledgment.

I smiled, and nodded.

– ❖ –

This is not a chapter about macho behavior. It's not a chapter about driving etiquette or controlling one's temper.

It's a chapter about choices. Choices: how to view a situation. How to respond to another's behavior. And how to understand, how to interpret, a particular event.

And I'll add yet another concept to the equation. A concept that really should be included in everyone's vocabulary: It's the word *reframing*.

I like that word. I learned it from my wife, who uses it in her psychotherapy practice. It can be extremely helpful in suggesting that a situation, an event, a problem, or a challenge may be viewed and understood in a variety of ways. When faced with a dilemma, we often see it from only one point of view, with only traditional options, none of which may be satisfactory.

Reframing is the creative and very helpful process of looking at something in a different light, from a very different perspective. And with that change in perspective come different solutions.

The decision to respond to a macho challenge by the inventive use of diversion and humor — paying a toll — serves as one example of how an encounter may be reframed, how it can be redirected in a totally new, healthier way. (And keeping the automobile analogy alive for another moment, lest you think I'm "tooting my own horn" with this illustration, believe me, the times I ended up doing the clever, right thing at just the right moment are memorable primarily because they are so few and far between.)

In our journeys through life, sometimes skipping, sometimes slogging, reframing can become an invaluable tool.

Consider the woman who grew up as the daughter of a full-time working mother and who, all through her childhood, felt an oppressive sense of regret, abandonment, self-pity, over the fact that whenever she looked out at the audience listening to her band concerts, whenever she participated in a sporting event, whenever chaperones accompanied school trips, other kids' mothers usually seemed to have the time to attend, but her mother, except on rare occasions, was always missing.

For years, decades, her mother's absence, her mother's perceived indifference, her mother's neglect, weighed heavily on this woman. Resentment invaded her relationship with her mother, and she just could not muster the generosity of spirit to forgive her.

Until the daughter had a revelation of sorts. A reframing. It was at that point that she realized her mother had made difficult choices, painful choices born not out of malice but out of love.

Her mother worked long hours to earn money so that her daughter could dress in clothes that would not embarrass her among her peers. She decided to work so that her daughter could attend dancing lessons with her friends and not feel left out, could go to summer camp and not spend lonesome summers in the city, could have proper dental work that would enable her to smile her stunning smile without a second thought.

The daughter began to understand her mother in a totally different perspective. And through this reframing, instead of resenting her mother, she began to appreciate her.

Same daughter. Same mother. Same history. Changed understanding. And it meant all the difference in the world for these two women and their relationship.

Another example: A woman I know had a mastectomy years ago. After the usual rounds of subsequent treatment, her doctors gave her a very hopeful prognosis. But, of course, there's always that lingering dark cloud hovering overhead.

Each person faces critical illness in different ways. My friend coped as well as one can with the shock of the discovery of breast cancer and the terrible anxiety that accompanied her every step of the way. She was able to deal successfully with the pain, with the side effects of her treatment. It was the scar that threw her for a loop. For years she felt mortified by that scar, inadequate, imperfect.

Until one day a very smart person helped my friend reframe the scar. Helped her derive a very different perception of the meaning of the scar. "You're a strong woman," the smart person told her. "You fought your illness like a tiger. You worked incredibly hard to help your family through this crisis. You conquered your fear and didn't allow the cancer to slow the rhythms of your life. You are left with a scar.

"Can you, perhaps, think of that scar as a badge of courage?"

A badge of courage. It may not work for some women,

but that's how my friend now understands her scar. She reframed her perception, and it has made a world of difference.

— ❖ —

Reframing is a private, individual task: It is based on a creative alteration of one's understanding of a situation, not modification of somebody else's behavior or feelings. Reframing is something we do in the quiet holiness of our own hearts. It requires a thirst for insight. It insists on an openness to very new ideas. It mandates willingness to change.

And reframing often requires some real courage. It's easy to try to change others. It's much more difficult to try to modify the way we perceive the world. But what a healthy, helpful exercise!

One in which the world won't change at all.

But we will.

14. The Doctors of Ministry

I'll never forget that day.

It was the XXX of Mai, in the year A.D. MCMLXXXIV.

At least that's what my diploma reads. It also states that the Princeton Theological Seminary has bestowed upon me the earned degree of *Ministerii Doctorem,* Doctor of Ministry, and that according to the faculty I am to be henceforth considered a *vir vita inculpatus fide christianus.*

A what? *Vir vita inculpatus fide christianus.* Two years of Latin at Classical High School in Providence, Rhode Island, raised suspicions, later confirmed, when I saw the full English translation: I was to be known as Rabbi Dr. Robert A. Alper, "a man of blameless life and Christian faith."

Who, me? You're talking about me? "Blameless life??" Well, maybe henceforth I could try to reach perfection. But the "Christian faith" idea did give me pause. Of course, I was very much aware that I was the first Jew in 160 years to receive a degree from Princeton Seminary, and the experience studying there had been absolutely wonderful throughout. I could easily forgive a Latin oversight.

I proudly framed the diploma, and on the back taped its English translation along with a quote from Lessing's play *Nathan the Wise:* "That which makes me a Christian in your eyes, makes you a good Jew in mine."

The events of XXX Mai began with 150 or so religious types robing together in a large assembly hall. The marshals gave us our instructions, and at the designated moment we began the procession. I'm always amused by the way people in robes and sashes and funny hats walk. Rather than a straightforward march, it becomes a sort of metronome pace, each person doing a scholarly tilt from side to side with every step.

My primary impression of that journey is that we traversed what seemed like 1.7 miles through the bowels of the Princeton University chapel, finally emerging into the rear nave from which we entered the chapel itself. And I remember that my partner along this walk was one of my classmates, a Catholic priest. As we processed, we talked about our plans for the future and recalled our days in the D.Min. program.

I told my colleague how nervous I was on opening day. We were a group of eleven, about to spend one day a week together for two years in intense study followed by additional years of independent work. Ten Christians. One Jew. More specifically, eight assorted Protestants, two Catholics, and one Jew.

One Jew.

That autumn day I drove onto campus and rolled down my window as I passed through the ivy-covered gate. I caught up with a self-assured looking fellow striding along the road. "Excuse me," I called. "Could you tell me how to get to Erdman Hall?"

"Sure. You're looking for the D.Min. classes? That's where I'm headed, too." At his suggestion I parked my car in a nearby lot and accompanied my instant colleague to class. We barely arrived in time. He had "guided" us to the wrong end of the campus, and only thanks to the help of two good Samaritans were we able to bumble our way to Erdman.

Three hours later I found myself walking back down the same road past the gates as, in groups of twos and threes, our class made its way to the dining hall for lunch. I was in step with the second Catholic, a parish priest from Staten Island. We bonded easily, and at one point, out of hearing range of the others, the thought was expressed, "Gosh. I feel strange here."

Only, it was not my voice. It was the priest's.

I did a mental double take, and then had the most calming thought: He feels strange here, and he's a Christian! Yup. It's going to be all right. We may come from different places, but we're all in this together.

And it *was* all right.

Interesting revelations kept cropping up. I spied a poster on a bulletin board advertising a seminar on "Intermarriage." This is a hugely important issue among Jews. Maybe I'll attend. Then I read the fine print: "An investigation into the issues surrounding marriages between Presbyterians and Catholics...." And I had thought we were unique.

During that first day's classes we got to know one another socially and intellectually. In the midst of a discussion I made a statement and the Lutheran minister attacked me. This guy is trouble, I thought. Straightforward, on the arrogant side. Maybe has some not-so-hidden grudge against Jews.

I finished the program in MCMLXXXIV, and have lost contact with all my classmates. Except for one, a close friend with whom I correspond regularly and meet for lunch every once in a while. The Lutheran.

I also became especially fond of a Presbyterian minister who, it turns out, lived in a Philadelphia suburb about forty-five minutes from my home. It was during the course of a class discussion of particularly difficult people that we discovered an amazing fact: Carl and I actually *shared* a congregant.

On Friday nights and on too many days during the week she appeared at my synagogue as a lay leader and very active volunteer. On Sunday mornings and, I guess, the remaining weekdays, she invaded Carl's church in similar capacities. Carl and I compared more notes: At the synagogue she stood about five feet two inches, and at the church about five feet five inches. Gray hair in my place, reddish-brown in his. Different names, as would be expected. No question, though: same woman.

We were certain because she always used the same M.O. A master of triangulation, this woman drove the two of us equally crazy. "Rabbi," she'd say, "you know I have your best interests at heart. That's why I'm telling you that *many* members of the congregation are *very* upset that you aren't attending all of the Saturday afternoon Bar and Bat Mitzvah receptions."

If I dug deeply enough, I'd usually discover that "many members of the congregation" consisted of this lady, her sister, and one of their husbands, none of whom particularly cared that I, too, needed to have a home life. And no matter how benevolently stated, the ominous criticism and career threat were there, making me very uncomfortable.

Carl would receive a similar broadside. "You know, Pastor, quite a number of the parents were *very* disappointed that you missed most of the Sunday School play." Carl tried to explain, in a nice way, that he doesn't exactly schedule hospital emergency calls to coincide with events on the church calendar, and sometimes he just needs to set priorities. "Well, Carl, I understand, but some of the people are very upset...."

Carl and I discussed our "mutual congregant" in a seminar one day, and received some sage advice from one of our professors on ways of handling people like her. What I remember most clearly, however, is our teacher's initial response: "Oh yes. She's the kind of woman that — well — you want to kill her. And then tell God she died."

Lunch proved to be as valuable an experience as the classes. Within two weeks we discovered better food off campus, and most of us would head for a restaurant where the roundtable discussions simply continued between bites. The topics were often less heady.

We were talking about the ways we juggled work-loads when someone asked about sermon preparation. Our Southern Baptist minister admitted that he devoted the month of July to writing a year's worth of sermons. After the hissing died down, one of the Presbyterians explained how he outlined on Mondays and wrote on the following days.

I added that I set aside Wednesday mornings to prepare for my Friday night sermons and Saturday Torah commentaries. One of the Catholic priests confessed to hurrying to meet his deadline late Saturday nights.

Our Episcopal classmate had the final say. "Well," he hedged, "I usually schedule a long hymn before the sermon."

The classes and the lunches and the occasional social evenings went by too quickly. Now it was time to separate. My experience at the school began with a walk down unknown pathways, and it ended in the same way, this time with a stroll through the labyrinth of the University chapel's basement.

My partner in the procession was one of the most serious of my classmates; for a number of years he had taught at a Catholic seminary. As we passed through dimly lit corridors between dusty, abandoned furniture, he became more animated than usual while telling me his exciting news: Just a few days earlier he had learned of his new assignment to become priest of the poorest church in his diocese. He was elated at the prospect.

The poorest church? The most desperate neighborhood? And he was actually pleased. Even more than that. He was joyful that he could begin to serve people who needed him most, and could soar to the heights of his calling.

I loved being a part of the Princeton Theological Seminary and grew significantly as a result of my studies. Yet of all that I learned during those years, nothing was quite as inspiring or memorable as the modest, sincere happiness of that priest as we strode along together to receive our diplomas.

15. Humanity 101

Is there such an emotion as "happy chagrin"?

I've never heard the term, but that's pretty much what I was feeling when my daughter was offered admission to all the colleges to which she'd applied. The batch of invitations followed four years of incomplete homework, unspectacular report cards, and dire warnings from an exasperated father: "You've got to buckle down and get some decent grades or you'll never get into a good school."

High SATs augmented by Jessie's charming, "in your face" interview style convinced all the smart admissions officers that this young woman had potential. They, of course, were right.

Ultimately it came down to a choice between the University of Vermont, often referred to as a "public Ivy League" school, and Bard College, one of the small, academically challenging "hot" schools of this generation. Both were excellent possibilities. I was delighted with either prospect, and relieved to have been proven wrong in my attempts at collegiate prophecy.

It was clearly to be our daughter's choice, but in one weak moment I couldn't refrain from pointing out to Jessie that her mother and I could send her to the University of Vermont *driving her brand new Range Rover* and still save money over what it would cost to send her to the very pricey Bard.

She chose Bard.

The school is located along the east side of the Hudson River, an hour or so below Albany. To get a sense of what Bard was like in years gone by, simply imagine a movie called, say, *Chevy Chase Goes to College*. In fact, Chevy Chase did go to college — Bard — and even back then the admissions people knew which kids fit into the prevailing environment.

Things have changed. Chevy Chase has not only matured, but is now a respected member of the Bard board of trustees. More significant, during the past twenty years a flourishing Bard has been transformed by its enormously gifted president, Leon Botstein. *The New York Times Magazine* did a cover story on this "most happy college president," and no article on successful higher education is complete without at least one astute Botstein observation.

I've heard Botstein speak on three occasions now, and each time it was an annoying experience. The first time was a spring "accepted students" day. Then the August afternoon when we dropped off our freshpersons. And finally, the October Parents' Day.

I was annoyed because, frankly, I really wanted to take notes but was embarrassed to do so. Lacking that, I wanted Botstein to at least allow moments of reflective silence between the thoughts he expressed. He's that stimulating. You just want to call timeout and ruminate on what you've heard. Botstein models a pure, uncompromising devotion to learning, a very modern educator and an old-fashioned Renaissance man all in the same person.

Some themes I do recall: Athletics? Botstein gleefully reported that Bard does engage in some intercollegiate contests, and "we always lose. No Bard student ever won a high school sports letter." The food? "We're not a four-star restaurant. We're an institution that concentrates on learning." Parents' responsibility? "Model intellectual pursuits. Attend lectures, the theater, the symphony, opera. Fill your homes with books and music and new ideas."

One issue he discussed, though, impressed me more than anything else he said during those three separate presentations.

It came up at the beginning of Botstein's question-and-answer hour near the conclusion of Parents' Day. That assembly was the one formal piece in an otherwise gentle, unstructured fall afternoon during which families became reacquainted with one another under new definitions, new roles.

As he did the previous times, Botstein lumbered down the auditorium aisle, a fairly tall man with curly, tousled hair, horn-rimmed glasses, and his trademark bow tie. He greeted a few people en route, then took the stage, grabbed the microphone, and began the familiar pacing back and forth that characterizes his lecture style.

A few words of welcome. A description of the topics he planned to cover during the hour. And then a digression that began with a request for forgiveness.

"The dormitories are really not in the shape we would prefer," he said. "A lot of minor repairs have been neglected. We're not pleased with they way some residences are looking, and we apologize."

But there was a reason. The president explained that a few months back a maintenance supervisor who is in charge of overseeing the residence halls was diagnosed with cancer. During the summer he underwent surgery twice. The prognosis was hopeful, and the man was now recuperating, hoping to resume work in December.

The college needed to address the man's illness and his absence. His was a critical position with important responsibilities.

What they decided to do was...nothing. No temporary replacement. No permanent replacement. No major restructuring of the staff. They would just shuffle along without him for a while, and if some things didn't get done, well, they just wouldn't get done.

The Bard administration decided that more important

than spackle and paint and squeaky doors was the message they wanted to send to this man during his battle against cancer. The message was clear and direct: "We need you here. We will not replace you. We eagerly, even impatiently, await your return. And we have every confidence that you will come back to us, in good health."

The assembly lasted another forty-five minutes. Other issues addressed have long since fled from my memory. But not Leon Botstein's apology and explanation.

Frankly I believe that what my daughter — and all of us — learned through the college's treatment of that employee was worth every dollar, every penny, of the tuition.

Whatever else she learned is, as they say, just commentary.

From Weakness to Strength
or Strength to Weakness

16. Unlikely Hero

"They rolled a drunk."

It's an old expression, evoking an image of pranksters propelling a tipsy fellow down a grassy slope.

The reality is more sinister, of course. Helplessness and evil are the major players in such an act, which is why our 1990s vocabulary refers to the "drunk" as a victim, and those who "rolled" him as perpetrators of felonious assault.

A "drunk" who has been "rolled" is not a particularly attractive sight. That was the report of the men of the maintenance staff at Temple Beth Zion, my first congregation following my ordination. They told me of the early mornings when they'd find Israel Starsky sprawled on the grass on the Delaware Avenue side of the building, his face bruised and his clothing streaked with dried blood from a beating he'd received hours before in the quiet darkness on the edges of Buffalo's nearby downtown. Somehow he would stagger the six blocks up to Beth Zion and collapse outside the entrance to that part of the building we referred to, automatically, routinely, as "the sanctuary."

By the time I arrived in 1972, Israel Starsky had entered a rehabilitation program at the Veterans' Administration Hospital. He had been an alcoholic for twenty-five years, and probably had attempted to confront his illness many times before, but this time he stayed away from drinking, every twenty-four hours adding a day of sobriety to his résumé.

He sat on the left side of the aisle, two thirds of the way back, always alone. He attended every daytime service and frequently came at night.

Israel was not an attractive man: His red bulbous nose,

rheumy eyes, and sallow face were part of the price he paid for his drinking, and his wardrobe consisted of one thrift-shop suit, a graying, frayed shirt, and a tie from another generation. As he passed through the receiving line, his sweaty hands trembled from his general nervous condition, and saliva often formed around his lips.

At one time, I learned, Israel Starsky was a top news-paper reporter, a bright, energetic, talented man with a wife and a daughter, a man who succumbed to the disease of alcoholism and had spent half of his life as a drunk.

The Talmud teaches a wise lesson: "Don't look at the vessel, but, rather, what's inside it." I soon discovered that inside Israel Starsky's abused and battered body lived an in-telligent and caring soul who had suffered enormously and who was trying desperately to regain his sense of dignity and purpose.

Israel and I had long talks, either in my study or in my car on nights when I would drive him back to his fleabag hotel. I learned that he spent his days in rehabilitation pro-grams at the veterans' hospital. But when he was not being ministered to, he would serve others, helping fellow alco-holics deal with their problems and tending to the needs of destitute hotel residents who would become sick and receive no medical care.

After Israel got to know me, after he began to trust me, he asked me to serve as his representative payee. The Social Security Administration, in an effort to make certain that alcoholics did not spend their monthly stipend on liquor, required that a responsible third party receive the checks and monitor the expenditures.

He was obliged to prepare a monthly budget and present it to me before I could turn over his checks. I still have one of his typewritten sheets, "respectfully submitted by Israel Starsky":

```
Income:
  VA Pension, $160.00. S.S.I., $115.60.
  Total $275.60.

Projected expenditures:
  Room rent at Stratford Arms Hotel .... $88.00
  Food ........................... $126.75
  Laundry ........................... $12.85
  Dry Cleaning ....................... $4.00
  Haircut ............................ $3.00
  AA Meetings contributions ........... $3.00
  Toilet Articles..................... $3.00
  Newspapers ......................... $6.25
  AMVETS Dues ........................ $5.00
  Temple Beth Zion dues............... $20.00
  Incidentals ........................ $4.50
```

When Israel delivered the budget, I reviewed it perfunctorily. After all, I knew that he wasn't drinking. I trusted Israel.

Still, one item caught my attention. "Temple Beth Zion dues...$20.00."

"That's a lot of money," I told him. "It's nearly ten percent of your entire income, and your income isn't very much at all." He realized that, but he wanted to pay it.

We argued. I tried to convince him that our synagogue was a socialist institution, with each person giving according to ability and deriving according to need. I reminded him that he was not required to pay anything in order to be considered a full-fledged member, and that given his financial circumstances, there was no reason whatsoever for him to pay full dues.

"It's our pleasure to have you as a member," I argued. "That's what we're here for. And nobody needs to know what amount you contribute." I even tried to bargain with him, suggesting that he pay a smaller amount, a token amount, rather than the full amount for a man his age.

Israel Starsky would hear none of this. To him, the synagogue was an extremely important part of his life, a clean, warm place, an accepting place, both a home and an institution of which he was proud to be a part. He would not change his mind.

Until that conversation my impression of Israel Starsky centered on his physical condition. Threadbare. Alcoholic. Ill. Unsteady. Anxious. Unattractive. Now I began to see something else. Dignity.

The months rolled on, and Israel continued to be a part of our congregation. Always alone. Left side of the aisle. Two thirds of the way back. Unless he was ill, Israel never missed a service. He would arrive an hour early and sit in the empty sanctuary praying by himself. Near the end of the regular worship, when the mourners were invited to rise and say *Kaddish,* the memorial prayer, Israel stood with them. He once confessed that he was saying *Kaddish* not only for those he loved and lost by death, but also for those he loved and lost through his alcoholism.

Perhaps he was even reciting the *Kaddish* for that part of himself killed during his years of sickness and desperation.

I wish I could say that I invited Israel Starsky into my home, that on his road to full recovery he became a close personal friend of my family, a grandfatherly figure to my children. I wish I could report that he reconciled with his wife and daughter, a healed, transformed man who began life anew after an emotional reunion with loved ones who never lost faith.

All I really know is that Israel Starsky left Buffalo before I did in 1978. He had come a long way in his rehabilitation program, and had remained sober for over five years.

He finally worked up enough courage to try, one last

time, to communicate with his family, whom he hadn't seen in many years.

Israel asked me to serve as an intermediary. I wrote a letter to his estranged wife and daughter, telling them of the progress their husband and father had made, and how desperately he wished to contact them. For years Israel had prepared for this undertaking, waiting until he was sufficiently rehabilitated to try to take his life full circle.

I don't wish to make of Israel Starsky more than he was. Still, just as there is heroism in darting across the ice to rescue a child who has fallen beneath the surface, there is also heroism in rejecting, day by day, hour by hour, minute by minute the liquor that the body craves. There is heroism in sacrificing meager resources in an effort to achieve dignity. There is heroism in attempting to make amends with people one has hurt.

The last time I saw Israel Starsky was the day on which I reported to him that I never received an answer to my letter. Later, I heard that he had drifted eastward, and was living somewhere around Syracuse or Utica, New York.

That was many years ago. I imagine he died in some broken-down hotel or boardinghouse or veterans' hospital, unappreciated, unacknowledged, unmourned.

But I will never forget Israel Starsky, because he was, in a very real sense, a man who demonstrated a kind of daily, even hourly, heroism that occurs all around us but is rarely recognized. He was my congregant. He was my client.

And he was my teacher.

17. Mittens and Gloves

This is a love story about Helen and Michael.

They were not in love with each other. In fact, I'm quite certain they never encountered each other, and probably never even heard of each other. It's a love story, nevertheless.

I usually write about people I know, intimately or in passing. But I never met Helen or Michael. I learned about them only from one of the things they had in common: Each merited eighteen column inches of obituary in *The New York Times,* Helen in March, 1996 and Michael the previous June.

Besides sharing the posthumous honor of being selected by the *Times,* they had a few other things in common. But first, the differences between Helen and Michael. And there were many.

Helen died at age eighty-six and Michael at sixty-seven. She was a Protestant who spent most of her life in Watertown, a small city in upstate New York. Michael was a Jew who was raised in Brooklyn and lived in Greenwich Village for most of his adult life. Helen married and had three children, eleven grandchildren, and ten great-grandchildren. Michael was not married.

Two very different lives. Yet their obituaries were strikingly similar in an exceptionally delightful way. It was their nicknames.

Helen Bunce was called "The Mitten Lady." And Michael was known as, simply, "Gloves Greenberg."

Mittens and gloves. That's what Michael and Helen shared. Mittens and gloves and a splendid, limitless love for people less fortunate than they.

Helen, her obituary explained, started knitting mittens in

1948, when a third-grade Sunday School class at her Emmanuel Congregational Church began to collect clothing for poor children. Her anonymous donations of mittens with matching hats and scarves sometimes totaled over two hundred sets a year, and were distributed to needy children all over the world. She knitted for forty-seven years, and near the end, in a nursing home, even taught herself how to work while lying down, in pain from severe osteoporosis.

Michael distributed gloves to homeless people in New York City, drawing his inspiration, his obituary explained, from his own difficult youthful years and from his father's wise advice: "Don't deprive yourself of the joy of giving." For thirty years, between Thanksgiving and Christmas, Michael roamed through skid row on the Bowery, passing out gloves to destitute people preparing to greet another winter.

"The Mitten Lady." "Gloves Greenberg." She contributed anonymously, but attached a handwritten tag with the words "God Loves You, and So Do I" to each gift. He preferred face-to-face contact, sometimes taking fifteen minutes to persuade a person to accept the gloves. He set a price, too: a handshake. "It's not so much the gloves," he was quoted as saying, "but telling people they count."

After a while both Helen and Michael began receiving help in the form of yarn and gloves from people all across the country. Helen knitted until shortly before she died, while Michael distributed gloves until 1993, when the cancer that eventually took his life forced him to discontinue his project.

This is a love story about Helen and Michael. Helen loved people and Michael loved people. It's that simple. It's that elegant. Two "little people" who made an enormous difference, not only in the lives of those they served directly, but also in the lives of those around them, those they inspired by their selfless examples of compassion and caring.

It amazes me how different these two people were: woman/man, Christian/Jew, married/unmarried, parent/childless, anonymous/direct — and yet, their beautiful hearts were interchangeable. I suspect that their stories, and their similarities, are far from unique. We need to learn about more people like Helen and Michael if we are truly to grasp the nobility of human nature.

It's unlikely that Helen Bunce and Michael Greenberg ever met each other. But if there is a hereafter, a place where people, or souls, get a chance to gather over a cup of coffee and chat, I sure hope that Helen and Michael meet up with each other.

I think that "The Mitten Lady" and "Gloves Greenberg" would have a lot to talk about.

And I know they'd like each other.

18. What Really Matters

My wife's voice. "I'm okay. I'm fine. I'm fine. But I've been in a terrible accident...on the bridge just before you get to Wallingford. Well, I'm here, and, um, well...you can't call me, so...just try to come up as soon as you can. But I'm all right."

Radio squawks and men's voices in the background. Sherri was calling from a Vermont State Police cruiser parked near the scene, her message relayed through the barracks phone and on to our answering machine.

I had been in Manchester Village, a few miles south of our town, eating lunch and doing mundane errands on an unusually hot July afternoon. From the supermarket, always my last stop, I phoned home for messages. You never know: Sometimes there's a truly exciting call, an important piece of terrific news requiring an immediate response. More often it's just routine business, or Sherri asking me to pick up a few additional groceries.

That day there were three messages in all. Sherri's call, a nervous-sounding young man trying to find a rabbi for his Vermont wedding, and the State Police dispatcher requesting that I call him immediately. Which, of course, I did.

He told me that Sherri had been involved in a crash on the bridge over the railroad tracks at the south end of Wallingford Village. According to reports he had received, an elderly woman driving the car ahead of Sherri had begun to weave, and then remained in the left lane on the two-lane road. The speculation is that she had become ill, perhaps suffered a stroke or seizure. As she rounded the sharp curve on the narrow bridge, the woman was struck head-on by a large gravel truck traveling in the opposite direction. The truck bounced off her car and into the other lane where it struck Sherri's car, also head-on, plowing our old Subaru into the guardrail.

The elderly woman died on the way to the hospital.

I raced toward Wallingford, twenty-five minutes north. About a half-mile before the bridge the traffic had come to a stop, and motorists ahead of me were standing outside their cars, passing information back and forth. "Bad accident. One fatality."

"I know. Thanks. I know."

Despite the oppressive heat I pulled my car onto the shoulder and began to jog alongside the line of cars and mammoth tractor trailers rumbling at idle. Just before the bridge, where the road makes a sharp right-hand turn, I spotted Sherri, sitting alone on a grassy hill in front of a farmhouse. We usually kiss when we see each other. A quick peck, a brushing of lips on a cheek, that kind of kiss. That afternoon was different. It was not a luxuriant romantic kiss, but one that was especially tender, accompanied by a hug that expressed everything both of us had been thinking.

Sherri was indeed fine, thanks to a fairly safe car, a lap and shoulder belt, and the fact that her automobile had received the second, rather than the initial, impact. She was fortunate, also, that the guardrail on the decrepit bridge did not give way. There was a thirty-foot drop to the tracks below.

"Thank God." "Thank God she's safe." "Thank God she's not hurt." The words, the thoughts, flowed effortlessly, naturally, through my mind. I was overwhelmingly grateful. A mantra of "Thank God" served as internal background music while we mechanically did the things that needed to be done: finalize the State Police report, locate the garage to which the car had been towed, transfer the contents of the glove compartment and trunk from Sherri's car to mine.

"Thank God." The frightening moments following a serious accident are not the time for sophisticated theology. More of the knee-jerk variety. Afterward I would begin to ask the kinds of questions I always ask. Did God save Sherri's life? If Sherri had departed from her appointment seconds earlier, might she have been in a different, more vulnerable location on that bridge? And what of the poor elderly woman who died such a brutal death? Was this also God? Or was it chance? Or poor luck? Or fate?

I'm good at asking questions. The answers sometimes come later, if at all. But inevitably there are lessons to be learned, valuable insights that can enhance our lives if we can discover them. After the accident, it didn't take long.

One of Sherri's colleagues was about to depart for a week's vacation. When he learned of Sherri's collision, he offered to lend us a car. He'd leave it in the parking lot of the hospital where he worked.

The next day we drove to the lot, where we easily spotted the car. It was evening, and the Peugeot was the only one there. Sherri opened the unlocked driver's door and signaled to me that she found the keys just where Charles had said they'd be. While she adjusted the seat and acclimated herself to the strange controls, I leisurely backed my car in a wide semicircle, to give Sherri plenty of room to pull out. I was deep in thought, intensely reflecting on what had happened the previous day.

I drove slowly. Nothing behind me in the rearview mirror. Empty lot. The radio was on and the air conditioner blowing, so I didn't hear the sound of the scraping along my right rear and front doors, or the gouging into the fender. It was only when the side mirror fell off that I realized I had backed my nearly new car into a three-foot-high Stop sign. Damn.

Sherri was unaware. I looked up to see her turn onto

the road and head in the direction of the restaurant where we were to meet for dinner. The damage was substantial, but after I ripped off a hanging mud flap and detached the mirror the car was drivable.

I started thinking, *I can't believe this is happening.* And almost simultaneously, another thought overwhelmed me. Jonah.

Jonah. The biblical Jonah who sat in the whale, or big fish, depending on who's doing the translating. But I wasn't concentrating on whales or big fish. I was thinking about Jonah's anger over the destruction of the gourd that had provided him shade from the hot sun. A worm destroyed the gourd, and Jonah, now exposed to the elements, went into a full-scale snit until God taught him a lesson in priorities. "You're upset about the gourd," God said. "Shouldn't I care about a city of 120,000 people?" It's all relative.

And it *is* all relative. For Sherri and me, two bad days. Two accidents. Teaching one very important lesson: Material possessions are interchangeable, but a life is irreplaceable.

– ❖ –

I pulled into the restaurant parking lot — carefully — and entered to find Sherri already sitting in a booth. Somewhat embarrassed by my clumsiness, I explained what had happened. She was empathetic. "You poor thing. Brand new car. Who needed this? You must be very upset."

I thought for a long moment, remembering the message on the answering machine, the conversation with the State Police dispatcher, the race to Wallingford, and my jog through the heat toward Sherri, sitting alone, uninjured, on the farmhouse lawn.

"You must be very upset," she repeated.

"Nope. Not really."

– VI –

From Health to Sickness and Back, We Pray, to Health Again

19. Getting Unstuck

I should begin by confessing that I *hate* high places.

I'm the kind of person who gets nervous when standing in the observation tower of the Bennington Battle Monument. That particular observation tower, mind you, is constructed of chest-high stone and small windows with wire mesh.

Yet I still feel queasy, nervous, and slightly off balance.

I inspect the roof of my house through binoculars, while standing safely on the ground below. It costs sixty dollars to have our gutters cleaned. This is not a problem. I'm delighted to pay somebody — anybody — to climb a ladder for me.

No need to drag out this confession. I simply don't enjoy being in high places. There is a word in the psychological lexicon to describe someone with my reaction to heights. I think I am an acrophobic. Or a wimp. I wear those titles without shame.

That being the case, why did I spend an entire day one summer walking down backward, and then climbing up, an almost sheer, 135-foot rock cliff — the equivalent of a fourteen-story building?

What was I doing there? I kind of wondered myself, especially as I was preparing to go over the edge on the way down; and I asked myself those same questions again when I was about one third of the way back up.

I was participating with a group of men my age in a one-day rock climb, organized by a psychologist as part of a documentary film he was making on midlife decisions. He felt that rock climbing presents an apt metaphor and marvelous learning device for challenge, change, and choices in life. I guess I qualified for the experience, since I am middle-aged, not physically unfit, and lean toward the introspective. And, I secretly hoped, because I'm naturally photogenic.

The climb had two parts: basically, gettin' down and gettin' back up. And I noticed that each part had separate themes.

Climbing down, or rappelling, a feat similar to holding on to a rope while walking backward down the outside of a huge building, primarily involved a combination of overcoming fear and trusting in both one's abilities and the safety mechanisms to which one is attached.

Climbing up presented a different set of challenges: While it also involved that same need to trust the safety mechanisms and the advice of the trainer who coordinated the climb, it also required problem solving at every step of the way.

Problem solving: addressing oneself to the issue at hand, experimenting perhaps, trying new avenues where old ones have failed, and ultimately moving on, upward, to the next and very different set of circumstances.

That's the secret to the climb and the lesson as well.

Imagine yourself on the face of an almost perpendicular rock cliff. Thirty, maybe forty, feet below you (four stories) is the ledge where you began. One hundred feet above you (ten stories, don't forget) lies the top of the cliff, where your guide sits, himself roped to a tree with a safety harness and pulling in your safety line as you climb higher and higher.

That's the situation, but it does no good to concentrate on what is far below or far above. Your immediate assignment is to move yourself twelve or eighteen inches higher, and sometimes it seems absolutely impossible. The stone above you may jut out and prevent you from seeing around it. To your left there may be just sheer, solid rock with no handholds or footholds.

At that moment all of your energies must be focused on finding a way, finding a place, to plant one of your feet, finding a grip for one or both of your hands, finding a niche in which you can rest your knee, then press on it as a way of gaining some leverage to boost yourself.

There are very few sounds. An occasional shout of encouragement from other climbers below, the constant rush of the stream down in the gorge, but mostly it's just the steady rasping of your own breath, a sound of heavy breathing comprised of exhaustion and anxiety.

It's not a terribly warm day. In fact, the temperature is perfect, but your hands begin to perspire, and the grip becomes slippery, more difficult.

It's strange what thoughts flowed through my mind: What in God's name am I doing here?! I hope I'll reach the top by four o'clock so I can call Sherri while she is still at the office and tell her that I survived.

A refrain from an unidentified classical composition kept repeating itself in my inner ear: Twelve notes, and then it started over again. I could neither control the music in my brain nor avoid the thoughts: There's no way up from here. This is totally impossible. I've reached a dead end and can go absolutely no farther. What'll I do now?

Of course, the answer is there is a way, somehow, to continue. It might mean traversing, moving sideways; at worst, it might mean somehow backing down, a very difficult maneuver, and then finding a new route. But most frequently, there is a way, somewhere, right there in front of you, or perhaps slightly off to the left or right; somewhere there is a foothold, a handhold, a way to continue the climb. The trick is to find it.

Looking to the top or the bottom of the cliff is of no value; only full concentration on the point at which you're climbing will solve the problem.

The cliff climb is a tough exercise. But it certainly is not heroic, and in most cases not a life and death matter. There is a safety line. It works. At one point along the way, nearly exhausted and with hands wet with perspiration, I slipped and fell completely off the rock. But there was no need to worry about a catastrophe; the safety line held (obviously!), and I simply scrambled back on to the cliff, dried my hands, and found a different route around the impasse that had blocked my progress.

And, yes, I made it to the top. What a wonderful, exhilarating feeling it was to climb over that last ledge, remove the safety harness and helmet, and scramble behind a good strong chain-link fence. I felt physically exhausted, emotionally drained, and enormously satisfied.

For the psychologist, that ascent up the cliff, that challenge to go on to the next place, to solve a problem, to move on to the next step — for the psychologist the lessons taught formed the focal point of the experience.

And for the rabbi, for me, that ascent of the cliff felt like a perfect metaphor for the New Year holy day of Rosh Hashanah, what we call the holiday of new beginnings.

It's a powerful message. The cliff climb spoke to me in so many ways. Being stuck and moving on. Understanding where we are, making changes where necessary, finding new directions. And moving on.

That is the theme of climbing the cliff. And most profoundly, that is the very theme of Rosh Hashanah as well.

Making change. Moving on. Constructing new beginnings.

We know it's part of human nature to get stuck, to be afraid to move on, to worry that there is no way out of situations in which we find ourselves, situations that bring pain rather than happiness. We get stuck. And unless we constantly remind ourselves that there are solutions, our lives fill with despondency and frustration rather than joy and well-being.

What does it mean to be stuck in life? There are many examples: Soon after that climb up the cliff, I encountered a dentist who, twenty years into his practice, aches for the opportunity to go into teaching, to spend his day surrounded by lively children whose futures he might influence.

Conversely, I also met a teacher who dreams of leaving the classroom behind to convert her hobby of cabinetmaking into a profession.

A surgeon who wants to be a concert pianist. A truck driver who wants so badly to work in an office: It doesn't matter what kind of office, just a place where he could wear a business suit and come home at the same time every evening.

I felt that same kind of stuckness, that feeling of being trapped, during the latter part of fourteen years serving as rabbi in the traditional, institutional form of synagogue life, and getting unstuck was a scary, then wonderfully liberating, experience.

Being stuck also refers to relationships: Former lovers who are caught up in a pattern of accusation and defensiveness, swimming together yet each very much alone in a descending whirlpool of bitterness, not knowing how to break the cycle.

An adult whose dreams and aspirations are still manipulated and controlled by a parent — or even the memory of a deceased parent — whose enormous power confines and restricts.

A young woman who, fearing an impoverished old age, chooses a profession that will provide financial security and foregoes a profession that will utilize her talents, her dreams, her visions.

There are many ways of becoming stuck in life, and being

stuck, whether in a relationship, in a career, or in any other aspect of life (including clutching the face of a sheer cliff) can be a terrifying experience, a depressing experience.

That late August day, as we stood at the bottom of the cliff contemplating our challenge, I heard the story of a high-powered executive who went up those same rocks a month earlier.

It so happens that about two thirds of the way up there is a large patch of poison ivy. We saw it from below and were told to try to avoid it. Well, this particular climber found himself unable to progress upward, and so he began to traverse, to move sideways, in search of another route. He inched closer and closer to the poison ivy and still could not find a way up. So he made a decision. After much reluctance, after spending many minutes — which must have seemed like hours to him — stuck at the same point, he decided to plow right through the poison ivy, traversing sideways for twenty or thirty feet until he reached the end of the patch.

When he got there, to his dismay, he found there was no place to go. No place to go but back the same way he'd come. And so he traversed, this time to the right, back through the poison ivy, ending up where he'd started.

He was unable to find another route. Ultimately he had to be lowered down the cliff, and by the time he reached his home, he'd broken out in a terrible case of poison ivy.

Getting unstuck is not an easy task. Sometimes it's very painful, sometimes we take the wrong route, sometimes we end up in a place much worse than where we began, scarred and battered. We don't always succeed. But that's the way it is with all risks in life, and getting unstuck does involve risk.

Frankly, whether up there on a cliff, or down on level, solid earth, I don't particularly believe in miracles, or some kind of divine intervention that will automatically rescue us from the perils we face.

But I do believe that people have an innate power to discover and utilize their talents and their resources. People need to trust in their abilities to find solutions, to come unstuck, to make change in their jobs, their relationships, their lives, when change is needed.

And as with the climber on the cliff, in real life, too, there are safety lines that will protect us from falling too far, that will usually shield us from hurting ourselves too badly. Our family, our friends, our larger community, the many other means of support that are available to us when we need them. If we falter, if we fail, our falling, our failing does not necessarily lead to devastation and desolation; rather, it can become a part of our history that builds strength, greater determination, and knowledge.

Everyone faces his or her challenges differently, with different resources, since each of us is unique. I made it to the top of the cliff at my own speed, in my own way. I made it to the top, felt that enormous exhilaration and relief, but also realized that reaching the top is not the end. There will be other climbs, other new beginnings ahead, as my life progresses in its unusual, interesting fashion.

And, oddly enough, though scampering over the crest of the cliff marked the success (and the very eagerly anticipated conclusion!) of the climb, it was a scary moment down below that taught me the most significant lesson. Halfway up the rocks, having groped my way to a place that afforded no more handholds in any direction, I tried to back down and move to the right. It was there that I lost my grip and fell a few feet until the safety rope pulled taut and I found myself swinging slowly but securely in the harness.

As I slipped, I let out a very involuntary, genuinely frightened scream, a nonsense syllable. Not an expletive, not a macho grunt, but a primal yelp born of fear. And a second later, as I dangled in the air and bumped softly against the uncooperative section of rock, I heard another involuntary sound: my own laughter.

Getting stuck. Moving on.

Fear, and then, if one is fortunate, laughter. Fright, and then, one hopes, exhilaration.

Life is, in a way, a continual series of challenges and renewals, defeats and victories. To avoid these challenges is to remain stuck, to meet a death of the spirit that is debilitating and just plain boring.

It's an interesting process, this getting unstuck. All part of the journey toward knowing ourselves better, toward attaining wisdom and a satisfaction that endures.

Getting unstuck requires courage. There are no guarantees of success. But frequently the safety lines do hold, and we achieve some measure of accomplishment. And even when goals are not reached, there is still one unquestionable reward: the knowledge that we tried, that at least we made an attempt.

And if it didn't work today, then, well, maybe tomorrow. Or next year.

20. Thank Heaven for Wisdom Teeth

The only problem with a kitten is that
Eventually it becomes a cat.

On the surface, the author of this couplet was writing about felines. But far deeper, I'm convinced, the poet had a very different species in mind. Teenagers.

The teenage years offer one transformation after another, one challenge after another. We parents who were once supremely confident experts at child rearing, comparing notes over ways we were increasing our infant's intelligence or channeling toddler energy into lifetime skills, now just moan to one another, eyeballs raised to the ceiling at the mention of the complex babyman or babywoman residing in our homes behind generally closed, often slammed, bedroom doors.

Although adolescence comes on slowly, it seems to end abruptly, usually with an eighteen-year-old going off to college or moving away somewhere. But in many households there follows, I've discovered, a pair of final transitional rituals: Thanksgiving of freshman year. And wisdom teeth.

Our house. Wednesday, the night before Thanksgiving. Around 9:00 P.M. It happened this way:

DAUGHTER: I'm going out.

ONE OF HER PARENTS: But, Jessie. You just got home from school this afternoon. We want to see you.

DAUGHTER: We'll be together tomorrow. Mike's back from Boston, and we're meeting everybody at Paul's.

ONE OF HER PARENTS: Well, okay. But please be home by one A.M.

DAUGHTER: You're kidding, right?

ONE OF HER PARENTS: Actually, no. I mean, we have a busy day tomorrow and....

DAUGHTER: Oh, c'mon. I've been at college for three months and stay out as late as I want....

ONE OF HER PARENTS: You're right. I forgot. Things *are* different. But look: When you're out at night, I don't sleep too well. I worry. So Jess...um...humor me!

A quick kiss. She grabs the car keys and is out the door.

And she's home at 12:30.

In our family the exchange on the eve of that Thanksgiving was helpful and defining. A guidepost along the path to adulthood and independence. Thoughtful older friends had prepared us, and we were not surprised either by Jessie's understandable priorities or our reactions. But that second event, the extraction of wisdom teeth, presented us with a most unanticipated gift that seemed to provide a graceful conclusion to the teenage years.

Wisdom teeth. I honestly feel that for many families, and certainly for ours, God invented wisdom teeth as a kind of round-about bequest to parents, like the finale to a musical composition in which a major theme is echoed one last time.

Think of it: In modern times our bodies have a number of superfluous parts. In earlier eras tonsils, appendix, gallbladder, and wisdom teeth all served some important functions, but these days they can be yanked out without a hitch if they're causing problems.

Tonsils, appendix, and gallbladder become troublesome at most any age, tonsils usually earlier, gallbladder later, and appendix whenever. But wisdom teeth are different. For some reason — a good reason, in my view — wisdom teeth most often become painful just at the time a young person is separating from his or her family, just at that stage when the child flies from the nest and begins to soar. Eighteen, nineteen, twenty. That's the age when wisdom teeth act up.

I'm now convinced it's all part of a divine plan.

Not every person must have wisdom teeth pulled, of course, but both of our kids endured the privilege. Zack's surgery went smoothly. Teeth out in the morning, attending classes at his college that afternoon. He was far from comfortable, but the pain was manageable.

Our daughter's experience was different.

Jessie chose the traditional time for wisdom-tooth work: the beginning of winter vacation, sophomore year in college, a week prior to her twentieth birthday. Early on a Monday morning I drove her to the oral surgeon's office, and ninety minutes later, minus four wisdom teeth, she was ready to go home. She looked like a slightly drowsy chipmunk, mouth packed with gauze, holding medication and several lists of instructions for follow-up care. We were assured that all had been routine, and that the recuperation should be quick and uneventful.

It was not.

(The queasy may want to skip this paragraph.) In retrospect we guessed that Jessie had a touch of the flu, or a reaction to the anesthesia. In any event, for the next three days she endured pain, nausea, and sleeplessness, while her mouth, which she couldn't quite close, continually oozed a combination of blood and saliva. One thing seemed to cause another in an unending cycle. Pain medication caused vomiting, which irritated the sutures, which caused bleeding, which exacerbated the pain and required more pain medication, which caused vomiting. All of which caused misery — hers *and* ours.

In a way, I loved it.

Most important, of course, is the fact that we all knew that this ordeal was temporary and medically well under control. The oral surgeon was reassuring throughout, and, in fact, he called us more frequently than we called him.

I loved it because for three days I found myself doing the following tasks: preparing ice packs, rubbing Jessie's shoulders, covering her with blankets and tucking in her feet, racing to the pharmacy for new prescriptions, giving her medicine, holding her forehead while she vomited, placing clean towels on her pillow, changing the soiled gauze that she clenched between her teeth, and wiping her face with warm soap and water.

And talking to her throughout. Not heady conversations. Just words of encouragement and empathy every once in a while. "You poor kid." "What else can I get for you?" "Oh, you're having such a rough time."

I felt so sorry for her. No parent wants to see a child suffer. But at the same time, I realized that something unusual had been happening during those three days. Reluctantly, privately, I began to acknowledge a surprise sense of joy and awe over an unappreciated but very splendid aspect of God's sense of timing. Who would have thought?

My daughter was nearly twenty. Adolescence had ended, and she was on the threshold of truly becoming an adult. A transitional moment of growth, a redefining of relationships.

Four teeth called "wisdom" took over her life for a few days. And for probably the last time — it had been many years since the previous occasion — I had a chance to comfort and soothe and nourish and reassure. Just as I did years and years ago, when she was a little girl.

For one last time, I was not her Father. I was not even her Dad.

I was her Daddy.

It felt very, very good.

21. To Baby, with Love

The worst — the very worst — moment occurred when they carried our baby into a "procedure room" where they intended to insert an IV into his head.

His tiny leg and arm veins would not accommodate the probing needles. The doctor had tried several times, unsuccessfully. Strangers' hands lifted him from his crib and carried him into the nearby room "where the light is better. Why don't you and Mrs. Alper wait here." We stayed in his room, but could still hear his sporadic, muffled screams.

Certain details I recall clearly, precisely. The look on his face as they took him away from us, for example. But other facts, important pieces of information, elude me. Maybe because the events took place in 1973. Maybe because we were so focused on our child. Maybe because we were so helpless. And frightened.

I'm not sure how old Zack was. Six months? Nine months? Over a year? He was little, of course. Preverbal. But I can't seem to pinpoint his precise age, or even the season of the year. Nor can I remember the course of events that brought us to the Children's Hospital of Buffalo. A middle-of-the-night emergency run? Or had our pediatrician calmly recommended we take the baby in for precautionary evaluation?

During his first two years Zack landed in the hospital twice — or perhaps three times — suffering from croup. This initial episode, though, was by far the most serious, and for his parents, the most distressing.

Croup comes on fairly quickly. A lively, happy infant enters a downward spiral starting with a cough that becomes progressively deeper. Then his voice mimics that of an adolescent male, fluctuating from higher to lower registers, followed by lethargy, watery eyes, and, of most concern, breathing difficulty.

Our baby was sick, sick enough to require in-patient care. During those initial hours we looked to the medical staff for their typical expressions of breezy, reassuring confidence but saw concern and frustration.

Again, the details are fuzzy, but I think they brought Zack out of the procedure room with an IV in his leg, and not his head. Away from the eyes of parents, the doctor probably made one last, successful attempt at finding a vein. Still, Zack was a very unhappy child, coughing, wheezing, and angry at being handled by all these strangers. They placed him in a crib covered by a clear plastic tent that retained moist air pumped in by a vaporizer.

I should add here, the doctors and nurses were not sadists. They were saving Zack's life, were as concerned as we were about his comfort.

The second-worst moment occurred later that evening. Back then hospitals made no accommodation for parents to sleep in their children's rooms. Visiting hours were liberal, but 11:00 P.M. generally marked the outer limit. Zack's breathing was improving, yet he was still quite uncomfortable, trapped in the tent with his hands secured so he wouldn't disturb the IV needle. He communicated, as babies do, with sounds and looks we understood clearly: "Pick me up." "I'm not happy." "I want a bottle."

A bottle. He always fell asleep with a bottle. If only we could get him to go to sleep, at least we could delude ourselves and depart the hospital in the hope that exhaustion would peacefully carry him through the night and our absence. But the nurse had no instructions, and refused. Once again, we felt intense heartbreak and helplessness as our baby cried and squirmed in his little tent.

Nearly 11:00 P.M. "I'm sorry, Mr. and Mrs. Alper," the

nurse said politely, "but it really is time to go. We'll take good care of him and call you if there's any change." Zack was miserable, and we could do nothing other than hope, somehow, he would finally fall asleep after we left.

As we collected our coats, I saw a man walking down the corridor toward us. His gait was slightly unsteady, not impaired but, rather, reflecting the rhythms of a tired, older person. It was Wilbur Fisher, our pediatrician. He had appeared at the hospital earlier in the day, soon after Zack was admitted. This visit, late in the evening, was a surprise. And at the same time, not a surprise. It was typical of Wilbur, an "old-time" doctor who routinely made house calls and checked on his hospitalized babies and their parents long after much of the city was asleep.

Gentle and, really, quite shy, Wilbur sloughed off our expressions of gratitude, examined Zack, and encouraged us with his evaluation of the baby's progress. "Wilbur," Sherri asked, "do you think he could have a bottle? It will help him fall asleep...."

Wilbur leaned against the door frame, considering his response. "I guess a little water would be all right. I'll place the order."

A few minutes later a small bottle of sterile water arrived. Zack began drinking with gusto, but he never finished it. He had fallen asleep.

When we returned the next morning, we discovered that Zack had been transferred to a different room. The IV needle had been removed, but he was still confined to the tent, into which the nurses had placed a few toys. This small, private room adjoined another, with a clear glass wall between them.

The child next door was six, possibly seven, years old. She sat up in her bed playing with a game, a small, very puffy little girl, who, we learned, suffered from a severe kidney problem that required isolation: no visitors other than properly scrubbed and dressed staff or family. Our brief inquiries about her were met with glum looks, downcast eyes, and a slight nod of the head suggesting that the little girl's prognosis was truly grim. Her mother stopped in several times during the day. We waved to the child and to the mother through the glass, but never spoke. We still had a very sick, very uncomfortable baby to attend.

Comparisons were inevitable. Zack was suffering, but he was going to recover. Unlike the poor child behind the glass. Zack would come home in a day or two. Unlike the poor child behind the glass. We felt burdened and blessed at the very same time.

The little girl spent most of the time alone, much of it sitting cross-legged on her bed, playing with toys, but frequently she peered through the window at Zack. Especially when we were out of the room. We'd return to find her trying to entertain him with smiles and funny faces and gestures that attracted and sometimes really held his attention.

Late in the afternoon, as we returned from a meeting with the staff physician, we noticed that the little girl seemed more animated than usual. Zack was clinging to the bars of his crib and crying pathetically. Seeing us, the concerned neighbor moved to a point just behind her door, in which there was another window, and gestured determinedly toward the floor, and then directly at Zack. We couldn't imagine what she was trying to tell us, until, assured of our attention, she signaled us to wait a moment as she squatted down on her side of the door and disappeared from our sight.

We heard a soft, crinkling sound, and looked down to see a wrapped candy bar being pushed under the low space and toward us. A quarter of the way, halfway, and finally all the way out, with small fingers wearing worn red polish giving it a final send-off in our direction. I retrieved it, rising to my feet as the little girl reappeared in the window. "Give it to him," she mimed, pointing in Zack's direction. "It's for the baby."

We smiled, thanked her as best we could, and tried to tell her that we would give the candy to Zack "later." She grinned, climbed back on her bed, and resumed reading a comic book.

Sherri and I walked over to Zack's crib and stood there, looking at each other, nearly breathless. In a quiet little corner of the eighth floor of the Children's Hospital of Buffalo we had witnessed an act of generosity so magnificent it almost defied description. This child, isolated in the adjoining room, dying, a sad, hopeless victim — it was she who raised our spirits, she who reached out to comfort our baby, she who cheered us during a fearsome time.

Our liturgy frequently refers to God as "the source of all blessings." It's a complex job, requiring lots of helpers.

That day, it was a little girl.

– VII –

From Offense
to Forgiveness

22. The Parable of the Knee

I think many of us spend an awful lot of time beating up on ourselves for incorrect reasons.

I don't mean to excuse the many evils we commit, the things we do, knowing they are wrong and rationalizing them away: cheating in business; cheating in relationships; bigotry; disdain for those who deserve our respect, and avoidance of those who deserve our compassion.

These are just a few. Our list of sins committed both as individuals and as a community is long.

What I am referring to are other errors, other poor choices we may have made in life, choices for which we feel a continual, nagging remorse at best, self-loathing at worst. If not viewed in a proper context, these errors get in our way, clog our vision, and most destructive of all, prevent us from addressing the current, correctable patterns that sour our lives.

Some of these choices for which we may feel intense, debilitating remorse include the selection of a spouse, a career, a place to live, the number of children to have. Business opportunities pursued, not pursued. Medical or psychological help sought or avoided during a crisis.

Think of it: When things turn out right, we forget about that choice process. But when things turn out wrong, self-recrimination, sometimes lifelong, often follows.

I remember an incident in my life during the winter of 1973.

I was a newly ordained rabbi enjoying my first year as an assistant in Buffalo, New York. One of the advantages of Buffalo was the close proximity of ski slopes, only forty-five minutes from our home. One Wednesday, my day off, Sherri and I hired a sitter for our nine-month-old and headed for the hills.

Sherri had some old skis, but I wasn't so sure about their bindings. Not wanting to take a chance, I insisted that she rent instead.

It was a good day to ski: not too crowded, with decent, though not excellent, conditions. Sometime midday we rode the lift to the top and then, as always, had to decide which trail to follow. None was very difficult, although the left trail was less groomed than the right one, on which we had skied most of the morning. "Let's try the left one," I suggested.

Sherri followed me down. But just a few yards from the top Sherri "caught an edge," as they say. Her ski went one way, her leg another. The binding did not release as it should have.

I won't go into all of the grim details except to say that, naive as we were, we trusted an emergency room resident at our local hospital when he told us to go home and return two days later to see the orthopedist. When we did, the man took one look at Sherri's knee, admitted her to the hospital immediately, and operated the next day.

She was in the hospital for a week, followed by months in a hip-to-toe cast, more months of very painful and, it turns out, worthless physical therapy, and finally, additional corrective surgery by another orthopedic surgeon and a twenty-seven-day hospital stay.

Many more difficult and painful consequences were to follow, some to this day.

When I look back at this time, what I always feel is remorse, even anger at myself. I chose wrong. I shouldn't have insisted on renting skis. I should have followed the easier, better-groomed slope. How different things would be. And why did we go to a neighborhood hospital instead of a teaching hospital? And we should have demanded to see an orthopedist immediately. When things were not improving during therapy, we should have sought a second opinion. The list continues. So many wrong choices. So many moments of bad judgment.

But then, when I look back sensibly, I need to remind myself, I didn't choose the wrong slope out of malice. As to doctors and hospitals — we did what we thought was best. We had no idea how serious the injury was, no way of knowing that a specialist was needed, no way to predict how inept the emergency room physician would be.

We did our best. We were wrong. But not intentionally.

And I think that's how many "mistakes" must be viewed if we are to move ahead in life. A bad marriage? Can we allow that we may have been naive? Poor choice of career? Can we understand that sometimes we are unable to control the marketplace, or that professions themselves change dramatically as we enter new eras? Styles of child rearing, choice of neighborhoods, friendship circles?

Who ever said we were omniscient?

23. A Second Chance

One Father's Day morning, the story goes, a young minister, a brand-new, first-time daddy, launched what he announced would be a series of annual sermons called "Ten Commandments for Effective Parenting."

Later, when he and his wife found themselves coping with two toddlers and a second grader, he modified the title to read, "Ten Suggestions for Effective Parenting," and by the time all the children were in elementary school, the sermon had been renamed "Effective Parenting: A Possibility?"

When his kids became teenagers, the minister dropped the series.

The fact is, parenting teenagers is a very tough, challenging task, and not the least bit glamorous. It's a serious, occasionally scary business, a maelstrom of love and ambivalence and testing and limits and pulling away as a child appropriately seeks independence. Along the way there's pain, anger, frustration, mistakes — lots of mistakes — and once in a while, a rainbow.

This is a story about a rainbow.

On Memorial Day Weekend, 1988, our son got into trouble. Major trouble. The kind of trouble parents don't particularly want others to know about, a crisis that I wouldn't write about, even years later, without Zack's permission. The healing passage of time and a college diploma have helped to mollify the hurt and embarrassment. And besides, there's that rainbow to tell about.

Zack was completing the tenth grade at a posh private school to which we had sent him on the advice of the experts. It was a struggle for us financially, a step in a direction we had never even considered, but after a few years of underachievement in the public schools, the prospect of smaller classes and stronger supervision in a more intimate setting offered what we hoped would be a positive solution. Zack is a sweet, funny, bright, compassionate person, but not competitive, a definite handicap in the Philadelphia suburb where we lived.

He wasn't particularly happy at the private school, unable to break into the cliques, but he developed a few friends and seemed to adjust as the year wore on.

That Saturday night at the end of May he had just returned from a concert when, somehow, a paper fell out of his pocket. It appeared to be a final examination. "What is this?" I asked. Zack looked at the ceiling and walls for help, then offered, "It's a sample test the teacher gave us for practice."

Family conference.

It wasn't a sample. It was the genuine article, lifted from the instructor's open briefcase when the man was out of the room. Sherri and I offered Zack only one option: The next morning he was to call the teacher, explain exactly what he had done, and apologize.

The teacher was gracious. He was pleased to learn the fate of at least one test. Many others, it turns out, had also disappeared.

On Tuesday the sophomore class gathered in an assembly where the full story of the purloined tests was discussed in detail. The faculty members announced that fourteen exams were missing, and requested that the guilty parties reveal themselves. Nobody did.

Without mentioning Zack by name, reference was made to one student who stole an exam but confessed and apologized. A praiseworthy act. The right thing to do. A laudable example.

The next day the school expelled our son.

Well, technically it was not an expulsion. Sherri and I sat

dumbfounded in the headmaster's office as he explained in a slick, corporate style that Zack would be given a chance to "withdraw" so that the dismissal would not appear on his permanent record. Very smooth. "You'll thank us some day," Zack's adviser, sitting uncomfortably off to the side, offered in what seemed like a scripted gesture.

Pleading that it was our son's first offense earned no sympathy. Wondering aloud why the boy who set fire to a meeting room earlier that year had not been expelled drew uncomfortable silence. "What kind of a message are you giving these children?" I asked in reserved desperation. "Confession equals stupidity? Whenever you do something wrong, just keep your mouth shut?" The headmaster presented us with papers to sign.

We were angry. Dazed. Humiliated. And most of all, terribly depressed at this demonstration to us, to our son, and to that school's student body, of the administration's inexplicable choice of vengeance over compassion, of what we considered to be excessive punishment over forgiveness. We wondered where we erred. In the choice of the school? In the academic pressure we placed on Zack? In forcing him to confess? That last question was the most haunting.

Forcing him to confess and ask forgiveness. We wanted to teach him to do what was right. The school seemed to be uninterested in the ennobling concepts of apology, repentance and pardon.

We were conflicted. Certainly Zack should be punished. He deserved it. But not expulsion. Later, we were equally concerned lest our indignation over the school's response overshadow our displeasure with the theft itself.

And lurking in the background, the question of what to do next.

After a few days I made one call, to the admissions officer at the Abington Friends School. I was nervous, wounded, well into my old habit of catastrophizing the worst possible consequences that could arise out of a difficult situation. But I decided that the best approach would be direct and honest, leaving no skeletons to emerge later on.

Carol Frieder listened as I explained the incident from beginning to end. When I finished, I probably held my breath. But not for long. Carol's words were transforming and healing, a verbal rainbow.

"We believe that kids deserve a second chance."

And they do. At least a second chance. The problem with the faculty at the posh school was that they simply didn't love my son enough. They had a different agenda, and a system of values that I still cannot understand.

Abington Friends was different. Zack went through the admissions process and in the fall entered his new school. He was lonely and ill at ease, he reported, for about three hours. It took him three hours on that opening day to realize that he had now, finally, come home.

The junior and senior years flew by and concluded on a warm spring evening as Zack and his classmates and their families listened to headmaster Bruce Stewart remind us always to be among those who respect human diversity. Bruce concluded his send-off with words that brought me back to Carol Frieder's statement nearly two years earlier: "Tonight, young people, you receive a gift from your parents and this school — and it is not an automobile, a trip, a pen, or a camera. It is a set of values! And they are deeply rooted in a loving family, and they have been nurtured in a demanding, expectant school."

For our family the turbulent teenage years have ended. The odometer clicked, and our younger child turned twenty. Both kids have left home — as they should. We really miss them. A sweet old cat and a peppy, somewhat crazy dog are not satisfactory substitutes.

When Sherri and I look back over the years, we realize that Zack and Jessie made lots of mistakes. Sherri and I did, too. Some tough times. Plenty of scars remain. There are things all of us wish we'd done differently, choices we wish we could replay.

But on the whole, with the help of wise, compassionate folks like Carol Frieder, I think we did all right. We're certainly pleased with the results, with the kind of people our children are becoming. I hope Zack and Jessie and Sherri and I can somehow forgive one another for the blunders we made along the way.

And I hope we can continue to love one another, now in new ways, in this new stage of our family's history.

24. Our Neighbor, Everyone's Friend

A few years ago there was a big brouhaha in our town, East Dorset, Vermont.

It seems that a tree company had been hired to cut down "the maple in front of the church." To the dismay of the entire populace the arborists mistakenly chain-sawed the very live old maple in front of the Congregational church instead of the very dead old maple in front of the Catholic church. The men felt terrible. We all did, and the story was the topic of rueful shrugs around here for months.

It was an honest blunder. The Congregational church is located in the center of the village, while the Catholic church sits back in the woods, up a small, quiet side road. "Remove the maple in front of the church" seemed like a pretty straightforward work order. Besides, who would have thought that a town of 350 could support more than one house of worship anyway?

East Dorset is a delightful little New England village. Few people have ever heard of it, which is one of the reasons residents love it. The most prominent name around here is Mad Tom. Mad Tom Brook, Mad Tom Road, Mad Tom Orchard. I like the sound of that name, and have fun imagining its origin.

A Vermont Railway track runs through the center of the village. An engine and a couple of cars pass by once or twice a day, slow enough that you can not only see the crew's faces but could hand them a McDonald's burger, if we had a McDonald's. Which, of course, we don't.

Hard by the tracks stands a town focal point, our tiny post office. Once a Long Island friend complained that she had to wait for thirty-five minutes to mail a package. I responded, "Busy day at our post office, too. There was another customer at the window when I arrived." The commercial district is rounded out by a wooden sign company, a car dealership, a motel, and the East Dorset General Store selling everything from gasoline to bread, all dispensed with warm smiles and the latest news.

In the other direction, east of the post office, are the town offices, the volunteer fire department, the two churches, and the largest building in the village: a bright red, rambling wooden affair prominently situated on the main corner across the tracks.

An old history book I found mentions that one of East Dorset's early settlers was John Manley, Benedict Arnold's half-sister's husband. I suppose we would teach this amusing historical footnote in our high school, if we had a high school. But we don't. Our kids go to nearby regional schools.

That same history book provides other, more interesting information, explaining how the town supported two churches as well as the role that big red building played a hundred years ago when life in East Dorset was far less sleepy.

Back at the turn of the century East Dorset boasted a public school, several blacksmiths, a cobbler shop, a cheese factory, two general stores, and two marble mills working in concert with the quarries across the valley on Mount Aeolus. Those quarries supplied the marble for the New York Public Library, among other buildings. A population mix of farmers and tough, gritty, hardworking quarry workers also spawned places for convivial relaxation: taverns.

The big red building was one of them, run by "Widow Wilson" and her son and daughter-in-law.

Now it's reasonable to assume that a small town is

not the place where you'll find earthshaking, earth-shaping events very often, but when I think about it, that's exactly what took place in East Dorset, Vermont, in that red building, on November 26, 1895. In a room behind the bar a baby boy was born to Emily and Gilman Wilson. They named him William Griffith Wilson.

A fairly common-sounding name. It may not ring any familiar bells for the average reader. But some will understand immediately when I add that he's best remembered as "Bill W." They know "Bill W." is a man who had sunk to the lowest depths of alcoholism by age forty. He was saved by what some call a luminous instant of insight and others simply refer to as a miracle. Soon thereafter William Griffith Wilson and "Dr. Bob," another Vermont native, cofounded Alcoholics Anonymous.

Born in a tavern in East Dorset, Vermont, Wilson still has friends all over the world, decades after his death. Members of A.A. refer to themselves as "Friends of Bill W."

In recent years recovering alcoholics, grateful for the transforming influence Bill had on their lives, repaired and reopened the big old wooden building, not as a tavern, of course, but as a welcoming retreat, a place to honor Wilson's memory. Alcoholics Anonymous members journey here from all over the world, just to say "thank you" to Bill W.

I meet up with visitors to the Wilson House almost daily in the post office or the general store. They're usually easy to spot because of the can of soda or cup of coffee in their hands. And the look on their faces.

The soda or coffee is understandable: benign drink replacing destructive. Their expressions reflect something very special, something that never fails to inspire me. It's gratitude. They have come to our town to offer their thanks to the memory of a man whose sharing of his unique way of overcoming his own alcoholism helped save their lives and helped restore them to productive living. They also visit Wilson's unassuming grave in the East Dorset Cemetery a few miles south. Wilson's small marker is usually covered with A.A. calling cards: medallions signifying months or years of hard-won sobriety, tenderly placed there by visitors, many of whom pray at the burial site thanking God and thanking Bill for showing them a way to reclaim their lives.

I don't pretend to understand all the complexities of alcohol or drug addiction. But I do remember how one person suggested I think of the urgency with which I crave my morning cup of coffee, and then imagine not being able to have it, leaving me with an unanswered physical desire that lasts all day long. That, he said, is what an addiction is like.

I see the Wilson House as a gathering place of contemporary heroes, strong women and men who day by day, sometimes hour by hour, win small victories that add up, eventually, to lives recovered. And they do this, many of them, through faith in a Higher Power combined with love and support from one another, all inspired by the genius of A.A. cofounders "Dr. Bob" and "Bill W."

– ❖ –

One of my very favorite stories from the literature of the Hasidim tells of a man on his deathbed, reviewing his life.

"When I was a young man," he recalled, "I set out to change the world. When I grew a little older, I perceived that this was too ambitious, so I set out to change my state. Even this, I realized as I grew older, was too ambitious, so I set out to change my town. When I realized I could not even do this, I tried to change my family. Now as an old man I know that I should have started out by changing myself. If I had started by changing myself, maybe then I would have succeeded in changing my family, the town, the state — and who knows? Maybe even the world."

I don't know if Bill Wilson ever thought of himself as one who would change the world, or his state, or his town, or his family. But he did change himself, and in doing so, and by sharing what he learned, he absolutely changed the world, for the better.

And it all began in a little room, just behind the bar, in Widow Wilson's place, East Dorset, Vermont.

25. The Saxophone Player

To: Chicago City Council
From: Robert A. Alper
Subject: Nickname

Ladies and Gentlemen:

I had the pleasure of visiting your delightful city during a December weekend and spent some time among the throngs of holiday shoppers strolling the elegant "Magnificent Mile." As I approached each intersection, it occurred to me that it may be time to change your town's nickname to one that more accurately reflects a typical visitor's impression. Instead of "The Windy City," why not call Chicago "The City of Really Annoying Saxophones?"

Inside the Loop. It seemed that the musicians were everywhere, at every cross street and in every sidewalk niche, instruments blaring Christmas songs and plush cases open to receive contributions from adoring, grateful passersby. Some of the players were halfway decent, and most of them, I assume, could also play other wind instruments like oboes and flutes. But it's the loud, scratchy, raspy saxophones that attract attention. They make perfect street instruments. They make me crazy.

I had a chance to play the saxophone myself.

At some point in his youth my father was a saxophone player. Oddly, I never knew whether he was talented or not, because I never recall hearing him play. But his old silver-gray saxophone stands out as one of those household treasures that a little kid like myself would investigate now and again, carefully opening the case and inhaling the pungent odor of metal and wooden reeds and green felt material that both cushioned the case and lined the mysterious air valves along the curving length of the instrument. By the time I finished trying to make sounds come out of the thing, I had usually broken the reed, but my father never seemed to mind. I didn't do it that often anyway. And I expressed no desire to take lessons.

I wanted to play the bugle. There was power in that instrument. And respect. Camp Westwood awakened to its sound, assembled at its command, saluted the flag, reported to activities, dined, swam, and extinguished the lights, all in response to the calls of Bobby Gormley's bugle. My eight-year-old logic convinced me that since my name was also Bobby, I could easily become Gormley's heir apparent.

When I returned home from camp, I announced my intentions. My mother, scion of a nonmusical family, was delighted with this genetic left turn, and immediately surprised me with a rented trumpet "because the dealer said you should learn trumpet, and then get a bugle." I feigned excitement, meanwhile feeling genuinely irked that I hadn't been consulted during the selection process.

I took lessons for a while but never became a trumpet player, thanks mainly to Senator Joseph McCarthy. Here's why: My teacher, Mr. Arthur Tancredi, a very nice man, came to our home one afternoon each week in an effort to mold the next Herb Alpert. But the Army-McCarthy hearings were on television during those very same hours, and Mr. Tancredi spent more time watching the proceedings than listening to me run scales.

Twelve weeks into this arrangement the instrument rental period expired. My parents were faced with a choice of renewing the rental or making a purchase. I would have been happy with a bugle, but they went for a shiny new gold trumpet, and in a masterful stroke of guilt production, they traded in my father's old saxophone as partial payment.

I can still see them surrendering Dad's heirloom over the counter to the dealer.

So one can imagine how absolutely awful I felt when I didn't practice and eventually dropped the playing of the trumpet altogether. But I had acquired enough musicianship to win a place as substitute bugler at Camp Westwood. When I played, my "friends" would stand squarely in front of me, dramatically sucking lemons. I didn't think they were very funny.

Once my camp days ended, the trumpet was passed on to my younger cousin Tommy, whose similar lack of talent confirmed, once again, that Herb Alpert would have no competition from quasi-namesakes.

For years, decades, I didn't think much about saxophones until that December afternoon walking along Chicago's screaky streets. Then, a few months later, I came face-to-face with a huge version of the instrument. Face-to-face, literally.

It happened on a Saturday night in Manhattan. I had officiated at a wedding at a historic hall somewhere in the financial district and was riding the subway uptown to my cousin's apartment, where my family awaited me. A pleasant spring evening, around eight-thirty. The swaying car was half full with the usual New York assortment of ages and races and ethnic backgrounds. Readers, sleepers, loquacious teenagers, and a pretty boring-looking guy — me — in a suit and tie, all bouncing along minding our own business.

He entered the car through the connecting door. Probably had been on the next car for a while and now decided to bless us with his presence. He was most likely in his twenties, although it was hard to tell his age or even see his dark brown face beneath a full head of long, orange-brown dreadlocks flying out in different directions. The car had picked up speed, making it difficult for him to negotiate the aisle. A drunk? On drugs? Or did his tipsy movements reflect the natural difficulty one would encounter when attempting to walk a shaky path while carrying a satchel in one hand and in the other a very large saxophone?

He stopped directly in front of where I was sitting and regained his balance by taking a wide stance. The bag stored safely between his feet, he looked around briefly, then raised the instrument to his lips. My face — my ears, to be specific — were no more than eighteen inches from the business end of the sax.

He began to play. Surprisingly sweet music? Mellow? Plaintive and evocative? No. It was horrendous. I had hoped for an undiscovered Kenny G. Instead, we were treated to a woodwind version of Canada geese en route to Fort Lauderdale.

As the shrieks of the instrument monopolized the train, the passengers began speaking to one another with their eyes. Downcast eyes, sideward glances, disgusted looks, resigned looks, eyes buried deeper and deeper in newspapers and books, emerging every few seconds to check reality. Eyes commiserating with one another. Eyes of prisoners, complaining to one another about their captor.

The "song" concluded dramatically with three outrageous shrieks. We braced ourselves, watching furtively as our musician slowly lowered his saxophone until it hung by its lanyard across his chest. Then he reached into his sack, grabbed an empty Maxwell House coffee container, and once again stood erect. Here's real trouble, I thought. Why couldn't I have chosen a different car, or at least a different seat?

The conversation of the eyes fell silent as everyone watched the intruder, tensely, defensively, awaiting the finale to this scene from the theater of the streets. He did not disappoint us. In fact, he amazed us.

With the slightest nod of his head and an almost imperceptible grin, the saxophone player called out just five words in a lilting Jamaican accent:

"Money makes me go away."

Here's what happened. People laughed. The books and newspapers and other shields fell into laps. One voice, soon joined by others, began calling gleefully, "More. Play some more!" Change purses and wallets opened willingly, and the coffee can was soon brimming with green as the musician completed his circumnavigation of the car. Stranger spoke to stranger, extolling the brilliance of our shared drama and its orchestrator. For forty-five seconds, we were a special community, astonished, smiling, relaxed, intoxicated with unexpected joy from a most unexpected source.

The subway pulled into the next station. The saxophone player replaced his coffee can in his bag, gathered his belongings, and walked onto the platform with the departing passengers. Others entered the car, took their seats, and began to read their papers or sleep or talk softly with their companions. The train lurched forward.

The entire drama took four minutes. But here's what also happened: When I arrived at my cousin's apartment, I had a marvelous story to tell, a funny story that set the tone for a very enjoyable evening. I suspect that the thirty-five or forty other subway concert participants reacted similarly, all of us now amateur troubadours recounting our unique adventure that concluded joyously with the words "Money makes me go away!"

It could have been different. The saxophone player could have uttered words that would have left his audience feeling frightened, menaced, tense, bitter, invaded. And we all might have arrived at our destinations drained, agitated, bigotry confirmed, anger ready to be displaced on handy targets.

If one believes, as I do, that one way we relate to God is by our refracting the rays of creation, affecting the next moment for good or for evil, then the saxophone player's five words were, yes, funny, effective, memorable, but also divine. He became a partner with God, giving humanity a little nudge in a worthy direction. And like ripples on a pond, the positive influences of that small subway drama continue to flow outward, even to today, to the telling of this story.

Religious history is filled with tales of prophets and sages and saints, madwomen and madmen, scholars and simpletons, mystics and wonder-workers, all of whom are remembered for one common reason: They made special contributions to that ongoing act of creation.

I wonder who the saxophone player really was.

– VIII –

From Loneliness to Love

26. A Woman Named Elizabeth Badt

I have a thick and ever-growing file in my study: records of funerals at which I have officiated.

Each one is unique, of course, even as each life is unique. I've forgotten many, and will remember others forever: the young mother; the boy about to enter his teen years; the grandfather whose love of funny stories prompted his grandchildren to tell a few jokes as part of their eulogy. The tribute "worked." It was appropriate for this particular man.

I remember angry and divided families, and families that exuded love and support for one another. I remember loud, heartrending and, ultimately, healthy wailing and moaning during some services. And I remember watching as a son, a navy admiral, patiently and lovingly spelled out my words eulogizing his father into the palm of his deaf and blind mother.

These memories come and go. But there is one funeral I think of often, one funeral that particularly upsets me, even haunts me.

Her name was Elizabeth Badt, and I officiated at her funeral on the afternoon of June 2, 1988. It was a strange and painful ceremony.

Elizabeth Badt. That was her real name. You can look it up in the death notices of *The Philadelphia Inquirer*: "May 31, 1988. Elizabeth R. Badt of the Schoolhouse Lane Apartments Germantown. Daughter of the late Anna Badt. Services Thursday, 1:00 P.M. precisely for relatives, friends, and employees of the U.S. Naval Shipyard."

There's no need to use a pseudonym to protect the privacy of family or friends. There were no family or friends.

I officiated at Elizabeth Badt's funeral. And nobody attended.

She was a woman of about eighty, the funeral director told me. No husband, no children or siblings. She worked as a comptroller in the Philadelphia Navy Yard, but for the ten years prior to her death she was bedridden in her apartment, cared for by nurses. The funeral director had met her one or two times when he visited her apartment to make "pre-need" funeral arrangements.

Elizabeth Badt knew what she wanted: a brown metal casket with a spray of flowers on top; a service at the funeral home. Then burial in the old cemetery in a reserved plot next to her mother, who had died decades before.

And so we carried out her wishes. I faced an empty room as I read the traditional prayers on her behalf. The funeral director sat respectfully in the adjoining family room. Nobody wore the black ribbon of mourning for Elizabeth Badt. Nobody shared memories of her life, or signed the guest register, or lit a memorial candle later that day. Nobody wept for Elizabeth Badt.

We drove to the cemetery in a pathetic little processional comprised of the hearse and my car. The leather-skinned workers served as pallbearers, asking us, as they carried Elizabeth Badt to her final resting place, when the other people would arrive. There are no mourners, we told them. After they placed the coffin on the lowering device, the men moved a respectful distance away but did not immediately return to their other chores. Perhaps they wanted to see what would happen. Perhaps they wanted to lend a presence.

With the funeral director at my side I read the committal

prayers, and he and I recited the *Kaddish* prayer praising God for this life that has ended.

Now the service was over, Elizabeth Badt's wishes fulfilled. I began to walk away, but looked back for a moment to see the funeral director bending over her coffin. He snapped off a rose, kissed it, and gently laid it back on the brown metal box that held the body of the woman named Elizabeth Badt.

Strange, isn't it? I have officiated at hundreds of funerals over the years, with each ceremony unique, each set of survivors and friends unique, each pain unique. Some I remember; many, quite honestly, I cannot. But I will never forget Elizabeth Badt. Remembering this lonely woman has become almost a sacred obligation.

And so, once in a while, late at night when sleep is overruled by my attempts to derive some sense out of life, and death, Elizabeth Badt's sad ceremony of good-bye passes before me, and I'm reminded of the importance of telling her name, her real name, to anybody who cares to know it. Some meaning will be added to her life and her death if from her story others will better understand the value of family, of friends, of relationships.

Nobody came to mourn Elizabeth Badt. Nobody paid attention to the death of Elizabeth Badt. Except for the funeral director. And me.

And now, you.

27. A Child Comes Home

It happened every summer. Newcomers, transfers, home buyers occasionally accompanied by their realtors, would stop at the synagogue to take a look around. My ambivalence sometimes became palpable.

In part it felt like a meat market with strangers checking out my institution, checking me out to see if they wanted to become a part of us. The rabbi must smile solicitously, engagingly, convincingly assuring all comers that we will fulfill virtually every one of their religious needs. Then they will join the congregation. Increased membership means increased staff and programs, which require an expanded budget, which is based on attracting additional members.

On the other hand, I met some really nice people that way, and it was frequently heartening, encouraging, to welcome decent people seriously committed to finding their true religious home. That's why I became a rabbi.

I could usually differentiate between the true seekers and the convenience shoppers. The former asked questions about theology, ritual, social action, and the like. The latter wanted to know about Hebrew School car pools from their neighborhoods.

Ellen Simpson and Jack Jacobs were more focused than most. They arrived on a quiet afternoon in early summer accompanied by their children, Emma and Daniel, and bearing a list of synagogues. A transfer was bringing them to our area from San Antonio, and they decided to choose a synagogue first, then look for a home.

Jack, athletic and shy, entertained the children on the nursery school playground, while Ellen, loquacious and hardly bashful, toured the building and presented me with her family's needs and concerns. It was clear to me from almost the very beginning: I really wanted these people to join MY synagogue. Ellen and Jack were charming, serious about Judaism, funny and very much down-to-earth. And, oh yes, they casually admitted, they were scientists. Both Ph.D. biochemists.

Clever folks, too. Ellen had retained her maiden name of Simpson. When Jack applied for his new job, he reported that at the end of the discussion the interviewer said, "We'd like to meet Mrs. Jacobs."

To which Ellen commented, "I couldn't understand it. Why would they want to meet Jack's mother?"

They joined my congregation, found a home nearby and, as rarely happens amid the complex relationships between rabbis' families and congregants, Sherri and Ellen and Jack and I became real friends, maintaining that affection long after they moved to California and we moved to Vermont.

The years passed. Emma and Daniel grew and flourished, and then Nathan was born. There was concern during the pregnancy about his health, but he emerged perfect and joined his brother and sister as a formidable — and cute — little character.

Ellen and Jack felt blessed and grateful for their good fortune: fine educations, successful careers, a beautiful, happy, healthy family.

But they also felt there was a part missing. A need requiring a response. Maybe even a cosmic longing to fill a void in their lives.

I really don't recall their motives, even though we discussed the issue often. The motives, the reasons, are personal anyway. The important fact is, after three healthy children, and in the midst of living the American dream of a life, Ellen and Jack decided to adopt another child.

And they were determined to seek out a child whose chances of adoption would be minimal. Not a white, American infant, but a child from a third-world country who was older, who had been passed over for adoption as an infant. They wanted to find an "unadoptable" child and bring that child into their family.

They worked through a local agency, and within a short time they had been "paired" with "their" child. She was two years old, lived in an orphanage in Ahmedebad, India, and her name was Mudra.

Mudra. A two-year-old named Mudra. She became part of the Simpson-Jacobs family. Her picture graced their home, her presence was eagerly anticipated. Her brothers and sister prepared for her arrival.

But Mudra didn't arrive. There began a frustrating, almost macabre series of hopes and disappointments that stretched on for weeks and months and ultimately years. Delay after delay. Red tape. Lies. Corruption. All against the incredibly frustrating knowledge that this child, this little Mudra, was spending her precious childhood in an Indian orphanage while her family in America lovingly awaited her.

The adoption agency social worker, a realist, cautioned Ellen and Jack to prepare for the fact that Mudra might starve to death before getting out of India.

One delay was so grotesque as to be almost humorous. An Indian judge rejected the adoption application. The grounds? He reasoned, in his wisdom, "Why would two American scientists with three healthy children of their own want to adopt an Indian child? Simple. To do experiments on her. Adoption denied."

Ellen and Jack persevered. Through all the years they refused to abandon Mudra. It would have been far easier — and even understandable — for them to shift their energies to another adoption agency, another country, another child. But Mudra had become their daughter.

Expenses skyrocketed, frustration mounted, and often the quest seemed futile. They never surrendered. They were determined to adopt Mudra.

Then early one July we heard the news. Mudra was coming! Ellen and twelve-year-old Emma flew across the country to meet her at Kennedy Airport. They arrived in the East a few days early in order to spend time with family and friends.

Their days with us in Vermont were somewhat like being in a fog. Sure, the usual visiting, reminiscing and all. But beneath it all, the realization that Mudra was coming, that in just two or three days this longed-for, dreamed-about, fought-for child would actually arrive.

Ellen and Emma departed for one more stop in New Hampshire, then on to New York.

Two days later we got the call. From Ellen. Back in California.

No Mudra. She didn't come. A foul-up. Some kind of riots in her city. New immigration glitches. Jack and Ellen didn't know what would happen now. Maybe it's only a temporary setback. Maybe it will never happen.

Thus began yet another round of lawyers and social workers and international phone calls, all part of a quest to take a six-year-old orphan and bring her to the family that loved her and felt incomplete without her.

As we anticipated, as we hoped, Ellen and Emma's frustrating, fruitless flight across country in early summer did not mark the end of the story.

One day late that July our phone rang. It was Ellen, calling from California.

Mudra had come home.

Two days earlier Ellen had once again been summoned, once again was told that her child was on her way.

A rush to the Los Angeles airport. No seats available on

the last plane to Kennedy. Ellen begged, pleaded. Finally she cried. She got on the flight.

We couldn't get enough of the details. They met at the airport, orphan and stranger. Mudra didn't smile for an hour, but finally she did begin to grin, and she never stopped. Mudra knew what was happening. The older children at the orphanage and the staff there had prepared her, had told her that what they all dream about was to happen for her.

Still, Mudra didn't speak any English, and Ellen knew only a few words of Mudra's regional dialect. At the hotel Ellen asked an Indian worker to translate for her. The man explained to Mudra that the doll Ellen had given her was hers to keep forever.

He explained to this bright-eyed six-year-old that she would be going on another plane, but her mother will always be with her, and that when that plane stops, they will be home.

A few weeks later Ellen brought us up to date. Mudra, she said, is unbelievably normal. Strong-willed. Affectionate. Bright.

She laughs a lot now — actually, as Ellen described it, she chortles. She likes to ride the bike with the training wheels.

Mudra's health is excellent, despite the slight limp that resulted from infantile polio. Not yet able to speak English, she gets frustrated and goes into tantrums like a two-year-old. She is, as Ellen pointed out, going through a whole series of childhood stages in a very short period of time.

Ellen and Jack are realists. They anticipate the trials that lie ahead. An adopted child growing up in a biologically linked family. Dark skin, Indian heritage, uncertain genes. A minority in a minority. Once Mudra was able to understand, she was formally welcomed into the Jewish community with a Hebrew name selected by her parents years earlier and cherished, as if in trust: Leah bat Eleenah v'Yochanan.

Jewish tradition teaches that for those who save one life it is as if they have saved the entire world. Ellen and Jack, I'm certain, don't view themselves in such noble, global terms. But I do.

For Ellen and Jack, and for Emma and Daniel and Nathan, the long struggle to welcome their daughter and sister is over. What was for four long years just a name, a picture of a little child thousands of miles away, waiting to join her family, now has become part of their history, fading into insignificance as life moves forward.

Ordinary people doing extraordinary things. Inspiring others to selfless actions. Encouraging others to achieve their own heights. Giving rise to that precious human commodity called hope.

– ❖ –

When I think of the story of Mudra, there is one image in particular that remains paramount in my mind.

It was during that exciting call from Ellen only a few hours after she and Mudra had arrived in California. In her inimitable way, Ellen recounted the details of their meeting in New York, of their quiet time together in the hotel, and the greeting by the rest of the family at the Los Angeles Airport.

And when they finally entered their home, Ellen related, Mudra at first "cruised the place, looking for the other families that must live there."

We spoke for about ten minutes. I felt guilty, realizing how exhausted Ellen must be. But I wanted to know every detail.

Finally the conversation was ending. One last question. I had to ask one last question. Ellen's response has remained with me, the image she described will always remain with me.

"What," I asked, "is Mudra doing right now?"

And Ellen answered, "It was a long trip for her, and she just couldn't stay awake any longer. She finally fell asleep on the couch. Next to her daddy."

28. Between Father and Son

The Volvo Car Corporation should make me their poster boy. Especially after what I accomplished on February 14 — 15, 1995.

In a skillfully choreographed whirlwind tour I drove my 1987 wagon from Vermont to Baltimore, where I presented it to our son, who had flown in from North Carolina. The next day I flew to Newark, picked up a new Volvo at the dock, and drove home, stopping at my daughter's college, where I paid for repairs on her 1984 Volvo sedan. The combined mileage on the kids' cars totaled slightly under 400,000.

Baltimore was a natural meeting point. Zack and I would have relatively equal distances to fly and drive, and besides, we could stay at my mother's apartment. She was away for a few weeks, visiting a friend in Florida.

Zack's plane was due in around dinnertime. I left home in the morning, timing my departure so that I would arrive at the cemetery where my father is buried sometime in the middle of the afternoon. I don't get there very often; the way things seem to work out, I see my mother in places like Philadelphia, Boston, and Vermont, and my trips to Baltimore usually coincide with the Sabbath or national holidays, when the cemetery is closed. I wanted — I needed — to visit my father, and looked forward to the opportunity.

The new Baltimore Hebrew Congregation Cemetery sits on acres of low rolling hills in a quiet suburb far from the city. It's a beautiful, respectfully maintained place, peaceful and comforting.

When Dad died, we decided to purchase a double plot in the bronze section, where, instead of upright tombstones, markers are placed flush on the ground. The area has a simple, aesthetically pleasing look to it, with the uniformity of the plaques reflective of the concept of equality of all persons in death.

Driving alone that Tuesday gave me plenty of time to think, and the poetic juxtaposition of visiting my father's grave and then spending an evening with my son was not lost on me.

Despite my carefully planned itinerary I made one error. The cemetery was due to close an hour earlier than I anticipated. Winter schedule. Still I pulled into the gates with twenty minutes to spare. Enough time to stand by Dad's grave, say a prayer, and think.

I passed by the Holocaust memorial, turned left, and drove down the road for about a hundred feet. Dad would be on the right side, near the curb, close to a young tree. But as soon as I got out of the car, I realized there was a problem. It had snowed a few days earlier, and while much had melted, the plow had deposited high piles that remained along the edge of the grass, obscuring those markers, including Dad's, resting beneath.

I couldn't rationally understand why I began to feel a low-grade panic, but then there are a lot of issues surrounding death that I don't fully understand. The clock ticked away while I tried to push some snow away with my shoe. I uncovered one marker. It wasn't Dad's.

So what? Isn't it the intent that really counts? A dutiful, respectful son, I had come to visit and had no control over snow. At least I was there, somewhere close by his grave. Appropriate rationalizations. It still didn't feel good. Though I knew the words by heart, I wanted to read and reread the plaque that recounted his name, his year of birth, his year of death. A momentary, intense spiritual hunger. A hunger and a very frustrating sadness.

Mine was the only car in the cemetery, but in the low

light of the late winter afternoon I could see two men digging near some bushes at the far end of the next section. As I walked toward them, squishing across the damp grass, one worker moved in my direction. When we met, he introduced himself as the head caretaker. I told him my name and explained my predicament.

"Alper? Are you Allyne's son?" My mother, at age seventy-six, still worked part time as a secretary in the synagogue's religious school. "She's a lovely lady. Sure, I know where your father is. Follow me." We headed back in the direction of the small tree. I hadn't been far off; maybe ten feet or so. With his shovel the caretaker removed most of the snow pile. As he got closer to ground level, he scraped more delicately, and when he reached the bronze, he brushed off the remaining snow with his gloved hand.

He had uncovered another person's marker. But now he had his bearings. "I missed it by just a few feet. Your father is two places to the right."

And he was. Following the same procedure of shovel, scrape, and brush, the caretaker exposed Dad's plaque: "Norman Alper. 1912–1988. Beloved husband, father, and grandfather." I began to thank the man, but even as I was speaking, he gave me a modest shrug of acknowledgment and walked back to his work, turning only to ask that I pass along his regards to my mother.

I spent five or ten minutes there, alone. I really needed that time. No more panic or spiritual hunger. Instead, that peacefulness I had sought.

It's interesting how the same event can mean such different things to the participants. I imagine that if the caretaker even recalls our encounter, it will be as, simply, one of those times he was particularly helpful to a stranger.

But to me, our brief meeting that late afternoon meant much, much more. The caretaker found Dad's grave, enabling me to accomplish the purpose of my visit. I felt satisfied, and I think I made some headway through that long, complex, mysterious process of saying good-bye to my father.

Then I drove off to meet my son.

– IX –

From Joy to Gratitude

29. Life Doesn't Get Any Better than This

Unpredictable. Unexpected. Without warning.

We use these words to describe events like catastrophes, disasters, and accidents.

How about holiness?

"Holiness." The very word has a sedentary feel about it. Holy places of massive size and artistic grandeur. Holy people, often aged, contemplative, quietly wise.

Holiness seems to be the antithesis of the mundane, just as the Sabbath is the antithesis of the workweek. But sometimes, to our surprise, holiness can be discovered in the most unpredictable times, in the most unlikely places.

Like a dark evening on a grassy soccer-field-turned-parking-lot near the edge of the woods.

It was our son's fourth year at a camp called Farm and Wilderness in Plymouth, Vermont, and our daughter's first. F and W provides a nice balance — some would say antidote — for middle-class suburban living, a place strong on interpersonal values, respectful of nature, offering an opportunity for kids to flourish in a noncompetitive atmosphere, free from rock music and video games, hairdryers and television.

We had driven up for the annual Farm and Wilderness Fair, a daylong series of activities in which each cabin builds, prepares, and runs a game, a ride, or a food concession. A kid-made and kid-powered ferris wheel made of wood; a flying chair that slid along a high wire, pulled by a camper running below; eggshells filled with confetti that could be hidden in one's hand, then squopped on someone's head.

Homemade ice-cream, fried bread, Indian style, flowers and vegetables from the gardens, animals on display, all punctuated throughout the day by African and Israeli dances, Indian teepee raising, storytelling, crafts displays, and, of course, quiet visits, moments of relaxation for parents and children together.

The fair culminated with a wonderful square dance; the dell was filled with people of every age, all stepping lively to the music of the home-grown Farm and Wilderness Band and square-dance caller.

Then, after nightfall, the final huge bonfire followed by a friendship circle, some gentle songs, and the inevitable parting. And that's when something very special happened, leaving a lasting, magical imprint on my soul.

I should preface this by noting that at ages nine and twelve neither of my kids was a candidate for sainthood. Like most children, they were blessedly normal, which means they fought on occasion. Yet, as in any family, there are remarkably tender moments that make the hassles worthwhile, tender moments that add meaning and quality to everyday living.

Zack and Jessie accompanied Sherri and me to our car, and it was there that we said good-bye. We hugged one another, and then suddenly, but not unexpectedly, Jessie fell into Sherri's arms and began sobbing. Suddenly homesick — understandably homesick. Sherri embraced Jessie back and assured her that she understood how hard it is to leave each other, even for a short time.

We all hugged some more, and then Zack put his arm around Jessie's shoulders, assuring us, "Don't worry. I'll take care of her." The two of them walked away from the car and toward the retreating silhouettes of their fellow campers.

I stood by the car and watched them as they slowly

made their way across the large field where moments before
there'd been dancing and singing and laughter.

Now the field was all but empty, illuminated by the stars
and the final embers of the bonfire. Neither child looked
back, but I followed them with my eyes all the way across
the dell. Zack's arm never left Jessie's shoulders. They just
kept walking, farther and farther away, until, at the end of
the field, they had to climb a small hill. Jessie had a little
difficulty; Zack helped her. Then they cleared the ridge and
were out of sight.

And I thought to myself, as I watched them walk together on that clear, beautiful night — just the two of them,
big brother with his arm on his little sister's shoulders — I
thought to myself, *Life doesn't get any better than this!*

It was a holy moment.

Holy: a word we really ought to use more often, a word
we ought to understand better. It's a mistake to associate
holiness only with bearded old men, dusty books, sacred
relics. The word holy — *kodesh* in Hebrew — or holiness
is a concept that is eminently available to us, to all of us,
and the secret lies in the ability to recognize what holiness
is. *Kodesh* really means "set apart," "special," and there
are many times in our lives when we encounter the holy.
Holiness can magnificently bless our lives if only we are able
to understand how and when it is occurring.

Holy times. Special times. Times when we can think to
ourselves, with a certain degree of thanksgiving, Life doesn't
get any better than this.

The cynic might say, "Isn't that sad: to think that this
moment or that moment is as good as life is going to get.
Then it must all be downhill from there."

Not at all. For once one recognizes one of those special
moments in life, the experience becomes part of one's precious memory. Part of one's history. Part of one's treasure

chest of resources from which to draw strength at difficult times, fond recollection on other occasions.

The key, the trick, the challenge, is to be able to appreciate when those moments occur.

One doesn't need to be traditional — one can't be traditional — about trying to recognize those moments. Holiness often doesn't occur when expected; it often does occur when least anticipated.

Life-cycle events, for example: birth rituals, childhood rites of passage, marriage and anniversaries. Our culture almost commands that we look upon these events as totally joyous milestones. Yet many of these rites of passage are filled with anxiety, family tensions, and the gnawing pain felt at the absence of special people who did not live to participate. Holiness, of course, can and often is found during the formal celebrations we anticipate and later savor.

But more often, the special moments are events that simply happen; they just come upon us, out of the clear blue sky, and there they are: an unexpected reunion; a day on which everything just seems to go right; a toddler's first hug; an underdog's victory; the completion of a task well done; a pat on the back; a rainy Sunday afternoon with a good book, a decent cup of coffee, and a fire crackling in the fireplace.

Those who can recognize how special those moments are can be counted among life's fortunate, as are those who can reach out and grab them, label them as holy, and firmly insert them into their autobiographies.

Those moments of holiness are food for the human spirit, food upon which we thrive and flourish.

Life goes by so quickly. So quickly. And the older we get, the faster it flies. A journey, my Jewish prayerbook calls it. A sacred pilgrimage.

A roller-coaster ride of success and failure, victory and defeat.

And because our life's experiences are so mixed, so unpredictable, we need to take hold of all of the refreshingly holy moments, embracing them and weaving them tightly into the fabric of our being.

My two kids, walking across the wide field near the twinkling remains of a campfire, Zack's arm across Jessie's shoulders, the stars gleaming as brightly as the tears on my cheeks.

And me, thinking to myself, Life doesn't get any better than this.

Who could possibly ask for more?

30. The Glance

I call it "the glance."

In the hierarchy of life's pleasures, on the scale of what's important, meaningful, within the human family, "the glance" stands right up there at the top.

Spare me the clichés. Sure, I know about the wonder of birth, the moment of falling in love, the report of a victory, a conquest, a long-sought success. Those are nice. Very nice.

But they don't quite match "the glance." Nothing can equal "the glance."

A hot Friday afternoon in June 1980. The academic year was drawing to an end, and it was time for the Jarrettown Elementary School's annual musical extravaganza. Two big, self-assured kids, fifth graders, emceed the affair, presiding over an afternoon of a truly cacophonous band followed by solo singers and instrumentalists whose lack of talent never interfered with their earnestness. And then, of course, there was the kindergartner whose piano virtuosity was simply limited by the fact that his tiny fingers would reach only so far.

The day's *pièce de résistance* was the chorus. Fifty-seven magnificently gifted, musically accomplished children of grades three through five filed onto the stage with a minimum of fuss and murmuring, took their places, and faced the conductor sitting at her piano. On the left side of the second row, three kids from the end, wearing a formerly all white and now slightly spotted shirt, stood Zack Alper. Age eight.

Fridays were busy days at my synagogue. Weekends are always crammed with services and religious school and programs, and Friday was the time to make sure everything would run smoothly. That morning I tried to work a little faster, tried to attend to as many details as possible.

Over breakfast Zack assured his mother and me that we really didn't need to come to the concert. "I'm just in the chorus. I'm not doing a solo or anything." "Well," we told him, "let's see how the day goes." We both had every intention of attending, and we did.

The gymnasium was warm and crowded and redolent with that elementary school/institutional smell. We sat on backbreaking kindergarten chairs surrounded by the usual clamor of parents and grandparents chattering, toddlers making quick getaways from protective arms, and fathers comparing notes on their brand-new twenty-seven-pound video cameras. Hank Ferguson, the warm and amiable principal, welcomed the visitors and assured us that the afternoon would offer up a musical potpourri the likes of which have rarely been heard outside Philadelphia's Academy of Music. We braced ourselves.

One act followed another, separated by blessed silences. Then, finally, the big event, the culmination, the grand chorale. Fifty-seven kids trotted out from the side door and ascended the stage. Naturally, they fidgeted. But in other respects, they were pros: no chatting with each other, no pushing or shoving, and especially no amateurish waves to parents and friends.

As for the audience, all eyes focused on one kid and one kid only: their own. Sherri and I watched Zack, of course, knowing that he was uncertain as to whether we'd be there. The conductor raised her baton and tapped for attention. Seventy-one percent of the choristers actually faced her, and nearly all of them hit the first note, some a little sooner than others. And — we were off.

We were proud, of course. Zack seemed to be singing all the words and paying some attention to the music. Even though we sat toward the rear of the large room. I could see that he was actually focusing on the teacher every once in a while. But most of the time his eyes were darting about, looking quickly in one direction, then another.

Searching.

Then he spotted us. Just a split second. The briefest of moments. He spotted us, and there it was: "the glance." That wonderful look, that extraordinary connection when a child discovers his parents. Zack didn't stop singing, but we could see an almost imperceptible grin start and then stop just as quickly. His eyes rolled slightly upward in a similarly happy grimace, a "yeah, I knew you'd be here" kind of expression. Then it was over.

"The glance." A split second. The tiniest fragment of a life.

And it was worth everything, everything, just to be part of it.

Later, when the standing ovations had concluded and the performers were allowed to melt into the appreciative crowd before returning to classes, Zack accepted our words of praise with the modesty of a professional. Finally, he offered, "You didn't have to come. I was only in the chorus. I've gotta take the chairs back to Miss Gradwell's room now."

But the good-bye hug and kiss we each received was more than his typical afternoon quickie.

31. A Holy Privilege

"Watch," I said to Sherri as we peered out the window. "David's going to lock the car door."

And, of course, he did. Happens all the time. A reflex action by "city folk" unaccustomed to rural living where it is highly unusual for an automobile's contents to be stolen during the five minutes it takes for travelers to enter a house, embrace old friends, and listen to the hosts' observations on how beautifully the visitors' children have grown.

Besides, our dog Giddy was outside on patrol, sniffing, then urinating on the intruding car's tires. That's what country dogs like to do.

David accepted my teasing gracefully, then tried to parry with comments about the remoteness of our place. They had fought the holiday traffic all the way from Pennsylvania. By the time they drove up our long, steep dirt road, passing only one other house, they thought they had reached the end of civilization. "That's why we love it here," I said. "Wait till morning. You'll see what I mean."

In the morning Leah and David understood. Now they could look out the back of the house and see the meadow and the trees and the mountains stretching to the south and west. Picture-perfect America, Vermont is a good place to celebrate Thanksgiving.

We were preparing for an even dozen that year: four Alpers, my mother, Leah and David and their two cute but semidestructive midsize kids, plus three friends from a nearby town. Thanksgiving is a marvelous holiday, spiritually based, inclusive of all Americans, and still surprisingly meaningful as long as the malls can bear to remain closed in its observance.

We ate a light breakfast and spent the next few hours

getting ready for the early afternoon feast. This is how it worked: The women operated at full tilt in the kitchen, while David and I ran a quick errand. The women continued energetically to prepare all the food, while David and I installed the extra leaf in the table and brought some fire wood in from the garage. The wood-gathering took about forty-five minutes, forty of which involved a detailed discussion of garage stuff such as the operation of a new chain saw and the use of drygas additives during extremely cold weather. Important consultations but, alas, time-consuming.

Trying to appear overworked, we returned to the kitchen. "Anything else we can do?" "No, we're about finished. You can just relax."

Around noon David and one of his daughters and I decided to take a hike up the road to the sheep farm. Sherri and Leah joined us. It had been a busy morning for them; this was the first chance Leah had to take a thorough look at our place in the daylight. We put on warm coats and tromped out the front door.

Leah walked down the two steps and stopped short. "Ohmygod!"

"What's the matter?" I asked. Leah stared ahead, hand now on her cheek in a gesture of disbelief. "Ohmygod! Is that what I think it is?" I chuckled, but David looked concerned. Sherri and their daughter were busy fending off the dog, who behaves differently outdoors than he does inside.

"Tell me that's not a cemetery!" Leah said as she continued to look toward the stone wall fifty yards from the house.

"Leah, David," I responded, gesturing grandly. "Allow me to introduce you to our neighbors: the Bowens, the Edgertons, and the Daytons."

We walked across the brown grass and entered the cemetery through the iron gate. I began my tour guide speech, the one I deliver to most of our guests when they first discover the small plot, twenty-five-hundred square feet, sitting back from the driveway so naturally and unobtrusively.

Vermont is covered with small cemeteries like "ours." It's not at all unusual. There's another one, about a mile down the road, next to a neighbor's pond. They contain no religious symbols. Maybe that was the custom in the nineteenth century, or perhaps these simple, sturdy farmers just preferred plain markers laconically listing only names and dates.

The earliest grave, I pointed out, was that of Edwin Dayton: Born on April 10, 1835, he died a little over a year later, a not uncommon tragedy back then. My guess is that his parents lived along this road, in a house that vanished long ago, and they elected to bury their baby close by rather than in the town cemetery a few miles away. A decade later Peleg Bowen, age seventy-six, was interred, followed in 1852 by his wife, Polly, age eighty. Next came the Edgertons: Robert, age sixty-two, in 1859, and Abigail, age seventy-eight, in 1872.

Baby Edwin's father, Josiah Dayton, age seventy-five, was buried next to his son in 1879. Josiah's marker also lists his wife, Lucy, but with no date of burial. She may have ended up in another cemetery, perhaps near a second husband. There may be others buried in the cemetery, but tombstones no longer mark their location.

I'm really not sure whether, technically, we own the cemetery, though we do own the land around it. It doesn't matter. Even if we are legal owners, Sherri and I consider that particular piece of earth to be holy, not an object of anybody's proprietary rights. A village trust fund pays for some annual maintenance, and I go in with a weed whacker every once in a while. We're not at all superstitious. Or frightened. We think it's an honor to watch over a place like that. There's a lot we learn, every day, when we look out our windows and see those silent resting places of people who once farmed the fields up and down our hill.

We spoke about Thanksgiving over turkey and stuffing and sweet potatoes and cranberry sauce and green beans and what seemed like more varieties of pies than there were people. Each of us in turn told of something during the past year for which he or she was particularly grateful. Twelve different examples. Some lofty, some mundane, all wonderfully worthy. Gratitude is an ennobling emotion, whether it be to God, to other people, or to the forces and accidents of history.

When my turn came, I decided to pick up on the theme of the morning. I said that I was grateful that we had a cemetery adjacent to our house. Leah raised her eyebrows in disbelief, and some of the children started to laugh. Until they realized that I was serious.

I explained that I appreciated the cemetery's nearness because, more than anything else, it vividly reminds us that we're just passing through this life, and all we possess is actually on loan from the Creator of life. Sure, our safe deposit box contains an official deed that guarantees we are the sole owners of a few acres of meadow and woods. And we have a mortgage proving that we (and the bank) own a house. But not forever. Life is finite. For the Daytons. For the Bowens. For the Edgertons.

For us, too.

We're all just passing through.

I don't find that thought depressing. I find it energizing and affirming, because in a way, it makes each day, each moment, that much more precious. All we have is on loan. And our possessions? We're caretakers, just caretakers for a while, and then we relinquish everything.

I like to meander around in the little cemetery every once in a while. While I'm there I check the stone wall, the gate, and the ground, making sure the mice and squirrels and moles and birds who live out there haven't done any damage. I'll clip a few vines that may have overreached their boundaries and pick up branches that have fallen from the large maples growing at the corners. And I silently read the inscriptions on the tombstones; my way of saying hello. In a mystical way this great-grandson of immigrants would like to think that somewhere deep in Europe somebody is respectfully tending the graves of my nineteenth-century ancestors. Wishful, fanciful thinking, I know.

Years from now other people will celebrate Thanksgiving in this house we built. They'll sit in the dining room, glancing in one direction at the mountains across the valley and then in another direction, toward the cemetery. We don't plan to be buried there; we'll most likely go to our family plots in other places. But if one Vermont tradition holds, the house may still bear our name:

"The old Alper place."

I like that thought. And I hope the spirit of gratitude — for the house, for the meadow, for the mountains, and for the holy privilege of watching over "our neighbors" — will remain around here forever.

– X –

From Pain to Compassion
and Grief to Understanding

32. A Mother and a Daughter

"Carl's. That's it. Carl's."

We were on our way home from the Albany Airport, driving along New York Route 7 just a few hundred yards from the Vermont state line, when we passed the old boarded-up roadhouse bearing the broken sign "Emmett's Italian-American Restaurant." We tried to recall its former name, and it was Sherri who came up with the answer: "Carl's."

The building had undergone numerous incarnations in recent years, but I first knew it as Carl's, the bar "across the state line" where teenagers from Bennington, Vermont, availed themselves of New York's lower drinking age.

I may have gone into Carl's once or twice, if at all. My parents moved to Bennington after I had entered college. But Carl's played a larger role in Sherri's life. Carl's was the place her father stopped for a drink on Saturday afternoons on the way home from Albany, where he and Sherri and her sister would visit her mother. A psychiatric hospital is not a happy setting for a family to gather; the drink, or maybe the bartender's companionship, muted the man's pain and smoothed the transition.

The girls would wait in the car. Sherri was seven, her sister five.

For a brief glimmer of Sherri's life Dorothy was a warm and loving mother as well as a talented and creative educator, teaching the older children in the same two-room schoolhouse, the Hick's School, where Sherri attended first grade. On winter days Dorothy packed Sherri's lunch: warm soup in a thermos bottle, and inside the soup, secured with a string, a hot dog. Dorothy was intelligent, clever.

But by the time Sherri entered second grade, Dorothy had begun to see green wormlike objects growing out of the walls and vermin infiltrating the house. One frightening calamity followed another, all tempered, slightly, by the embrace of Aunt Liz to whose home Sherri and Pam were frequently rushed. Meanwhile Dorothy moved further and further into a universe of psychiatrists, neurologists, hospitalizations, electroshock therapy. There was very little time left for mothering.

On television the greeting-card industry and the coffee industry do it best: poignant scenes of average people warmly relating to one another during transitional moments. The kid coming home from college in a snowstorm; the gathering of an extended family for an elder's birthday party; the mother and her twenty-something daughter chatting about life while they wash and dry dishes.

The mother and her twenty-something daughter chatting.

In October 1971, I was completing my last year at the rabbinical seminary in Cincinnati and Sherri was working at a dreadfully boring office job. A welcome break in the routine came with a request that I officiate at a wedding in Vermont. The bride's parents would fly both of us East for the event, and they secured a local justice of the peace to co-officiate with me since I had not yet been ordained. It was a beautiful quasi-counterculture ceremony by a pond, with peak foliage surrounding us and a plastic Smokey the Bear atop the wedding cake.

Sherri wore her long hair in a bun on her head, the way I loved it, and an ankle-length dark blue dress with white polka dots. People remarked how beautiful she looked. I was the only one who knew the reason why she seemed to radiate. She was eight weeks pregnant.

The mother and her twenty-something daughter chatting. What can be more sublime than those tender minutes when a mother and daughter bond in a brand-new way following the revelation of a long-anticipated first pregnancy?

The day after the wedding we drove to see Sherri's parents in Bennington. Dorothy was out of control, paranoid, suffering seizures, staggering and falling, constantly injuring herself. Sherri's father had given up and arranged to be at work most of the time. There were no mother-daughter heart-to-heart talks. No celebration of the new pregnancy or maternal guidance or dreamy looks into the future. Instead, Sherri and I packed a few suitcases and cartons and delivered them, along with Dorothy, to a nursing home. Dorothy was fifty-three.

Six weeks after our son was born, we moved to Buffalo and my first congregation. At least western New York was a manageable day's drive from Bennington, an important consideration since Dorothy, through her verbal and physical confrontations with patients and staff, had embarked on a long series of nursing home expulsions, crisis after crisis that now fell completely on our shoulders. Sherri's father, probably more out of pain than malice, had removed himself from the situation.

After two years we ran out of options in Bennington and brought Dorothy to Buffalo, acquiring along the way two guardian angels in the form of hospital social worker Shirley Kloner and psychiatrist Gary Cohen. Dorothy spent months on Buffalo General Hospital's psychiatric floor being evaluated by experts from all disciplines. Ultimately Gary informed us that there was really nothing they could do to help her, that her situation was bizarre, unable to be diagnosed — in reality, hopeless. The compassion and frustration in Gary's voice gave us strength. Understanding how diligently he and Shirley and others had tried to help gave us comfort.

More nursing homes. More expulsions after Dorothy hit an aide with her walker, or flung a glass of milk at a roommate.

The nadir occurred in January 1976, on what must have been one of the coldest, windiest days in Buffalo's harsh weather history. As a last resort, we had placed Dorothy in a kind of "residential home" that offered some nursing capability, but they, too, soon telephoned us with the familiar ultimatum: "Come get your mother. We can no longer handle her." That horrible day began with the forcible sedation of a screaming and flailing woman and ended with us exiting the huge gates of a state psychiatric hospital, where, having run out of options, we had deposited Dorothy.

Sherri was crying. She should have been smiling. She deserved to have been happier. Just two weeks earlier she had given birth to our gorgeous, healthy daughter.

Within a month we were able to convince yet another nursing home to accept Dorothy, and the odyssey continued, nursing home to nursing home, upheaval after upheaval, first in Buffalo, then in Philadelphia, and ultimately back to Vermont as our family moved from place to place. Somewhere a few years back Dorothy developed a very rare form of cancer. The surgery would be palliative only, we were told; this cancer is definitely fatal.

It was not.

My mother-in-law is nearly eighty now. She weighs about eighty-five pounds, hasn't walked in twenty years, and shares a room with a semicomatose woman in a lovely nursing home in Bennington. When she isn't sleeping, she sits in her wheelchair, alone on her side of the room. She hasn't read or watched TV ever since her glasses broke. Sherri brought her a new pair, but Dorothy refused to wear them. "No," she insisted, "these are not mine. I won't put them on." Nothing could convince her otherwise, and rather than wear "someone else's glasses," she just sits and stares, and has done so for four years.

She recognizes people and gives a big hug to her visitors. She's much weaker now, far less belligerent, and has been incontinent for about fifteen years. Her speech is soft and slurred, often unintelligible. She still enjoys going out to Pizza Hut and is appreciative of the opportunity to drink "a good hot cup of coffee."

Our kids are sweet with her. Understanding and patient. Once, for an entire year, Dorothy insisted that Zack was not her grandson but her nephew Stephen. Jessie and Zack have no memory of a healthy, loving, giving maternal grandmother. So every once in a while Sherri tries to describe what Dorothy was like as a young woman, as a teacher, as a parent. It's difficult for Sherri. From age seven on, she really didn't have a mother. Inspired by and grateful to Shirley Kloner, Sherri eventually became a clinical social worker, a nurturing caretaker, providing to others what she herself had been denied.

Dorothy seems comfortable. She smiles once in a while, occasionally rearing her head back in an awkward grin.

But I have never heard her laugh.

One of the things I love most about being a rabbi is the opportunity to enter into people's lives during their times of bereavement and help them endure the harshness of those moments. The most important technique is the ability to listen. And so I listen.

Everybody's suffering is unique, but similarities exist. On many occasions I have heard a woman's agonized refrain, "How could she be gone? How could she leave me? She wasn't just my mother. She was my very best friend! Nobody will ever understand: We spoke on the phone every day, sometimes two or three times. She had such a youthful outlook. We could confide in each other. Oh, God. I miss her terribly."

I listen. That's most important. The story needs to be told, over and over again, if possible. I listen. I offer to hold a hand, even give a hug, although I am still awkward at this. I empathize. "Her absence must be so difficult for you. What an immeasurable loss you've suffered."

I say what I hope are effective words of consolation. I offer sympathy that is truly genuine. I internalize some of the hurt that floods the room.

And I am envious.

I envy their closeness. I envy the kind of history they shared, the memories that will endure, the profound effect they have had on each other's lives. And I envy the longing that now produces tears and sighs and anger at God or fate.

A strange concept, no doubt: to envy another's pain. But that sharp pain is the inevitable price we pay for combining infinite love with what is, after all, finite existence. Sherri will never feel that kind of acute pain for her mother. Hers is an enduring ache, a prolonged, throbbing sadness that becomes more vivid only when she thinks of the reality of her mother's horrible life, an emotional exercise she tries to avoid.

As for me, I pity Dorothy. I feel so very sad for the waste that is her life. And I frequently remind myself that of course . . . of course . . . Dorothy would never have chosen such a grim fate. Nobody would choose such an existence.

Sometimes I'm angry at her. When she's particularly paranoid and argumentative, or when her diaper leaks across my car seat, I think cruel thoughts and express my frustration to anybody but Dorothy. It's how I cope.

One recent November day Sherri and I visited Dorothy in the nursing home. We found her, as usual, sitting in her wheelchair by her bed, slowly eating the noonday meal. We placed the hot coffee we had brought on the tray, and Dorothy gave us her awkward hug, enough of an embrace to make me feel guilty that I did not stop by more frequently. I have difficulty understanding her speech now, so we just spoke briefly. Sherri engaged her in the usual conversation, while she wrote Dorothy's name in Magic Marker on the cigarettes and Kleenex and toothpaste we had brought. I paced around the room.

I watched the two of them, mother and daughter, the daughter who has for so many years been a mother to her mother. Sherri combed Dorothy's hair, told her some brief news about our kids. Dorothy responded, "Well. That's nice." In the midst of our visit an announcement came over the public address. The day, the date, the weather, and a list of activities.

We concluded our visit and hugged and kissed good-bye. Only as we walked into the parking lot did it occur to me that Dorothy had not repeated to Sherri what others had been saying all morning: "Happy Birthday."

My mother-in-law. One woman's story. No pat answers here. No rationalizations. Not even an attempt at an explanation, theological or otherwise. Just one word that comes to mind whenever I think of her long and sorrowful life:

Why?

33. Old Lovers

My mother and father observed an unusual ritual through-out their nearly forty-nine years of marriage. Whenever they left home together, just before walking through the door, they would kiss each other. Usually it was a perfunctory kiss, a force of habit kind of thing, but without question it was mandatory for them, almost like paying homage to a superstition, which it was not.

Apparently they had kissed at the door ever since they were newlyweds, and the custom held. Even if they were in the midst of a quarrel (and their arguments were always civil), there would be that brief pause, the kiss, and the discussion would continue as they walked outside. As a kid, I thought all couples kissed whenever they left their home.

Certain memories surrounding my father's death remain especially clear in my mind. The phone call, the funeral, the hundreds of people offering consolation, my teenage son's arm around my shoulders, and reciting *Kaddish,* the mourner's prayer I had led thousands of times, now as a mourner myself.

But most of all, I remember watching my mother leaving the apartment on the way to the funeral. When she reached the front door, she paused for a moment, only a moment, and sighed. Then she squeezed my hand hard, and walked out into the hallway.

I wouldn't dare try to characterize my parents' marriage. After all, what does a child, even a grown child, really know about his parents' relationship? But there is history that I experienced along with them, and themes in their lives to which I was privy. Lots of heartache and hard times, but also a good deal of joy and pride and a more comfortable life toward the end.

My mother and father often joked facetiously that theirs

was an intermarriage, and perhaps in 1940 they did qualify somewhat, Mom as the granddaughter of German-Jewish immigrants and Dad as the grandson of Russian-Jewish immigrants. Her ancestry was of the punctual, exacting variety, and his of a more relaxed, quixotic nature. Their two backgrounds occasionally clashed, as at the conclusion of a Thanksgiving visit to our home in Philadelphia.

Always one of my favorite holidays, this Thanksgiving we had enjoyed a large, festive celebration on Thursday, and now it was Friday afternoon with just Sherri, our kids, and my parents sitting around the dining-room table picking through leftovers. Everyone was feeling relaxed and full. My mother excused herself from the table, announcing that she was going upstairs to pack so that she and my father could get back home to Baltimore in plenty of time to attend Sabbath evening services. A few minutes later, the predictable call from on high: "Norman, are you coming up to help?"

My father, who in his later years had developed grousing into an art form, was annoyed. Not only was he annoyed, but this day he had an audience to whom he could ruefully complain, "Punctual. Always punctual. She has to be on time. Everything done on schedule. Very precise." (The final syllable emphasized through clenched teeth.) He was enjoying himself as he rehearsed the old theme. Mom called again, and Dad continued to expound on the qualities of persons afflicted with a German-Jewish heritage. The kids fell silent. Sherri and I became increasingly uncomfortable.

For one of the first times in my life — for I was still their child — I decided to intervene, and the device I chose was humor. I took a big breath, then looked at my father with raised eyebrows and suggested, "Yeah, Dad. She's a real pain. Why don't you dump her?"

Sherri and the kids did doubletakes, then began to laugh

hysterically. My father, caught off guard, smiled, pretended to agree that it was not a half-bad idea, and joined in the laughter. Even my mother thought it was funny, once we let her in on the joke.

In the final years of their marriage my parents experienced an increase in tension, sniping, impatience, and anger. I stood to the side, sad, hoping the same would not happen between Sherri and me, and wondering if what I was witnessing was unique to Mom and Dad or a natural by-product of the frustrations of aging.

Still, the psalmist wrote how in God's sight a thousand years are like one day. In human experience I learned that sometimes one brief moment can outweigh decades. One brief moment can become more significant than all the events and feelings of the years that surround it. A moment in a cold, formal hospital room, for example.

A few months after that Thanksgiving encounter my father entered the hospital for prostate surgery, a common operation for men his age but scary nevertheless. On the morning of the surgery he was slightly groggy but still cavalier when my mother and I kissed him good-bye. We ate a little breakfast and passed the time as people do in hospitals until the doctor arrived with a good report and the promise that Dad would be returned to his room within an hour.

We awaited him. Finally a squad of orderlies and nurses wheeled him into the room and carefully transferred him from litter to bed. When the people cleared away, I looked down to see a much older-looking Norman Alper, his hair matted, his mouth shriveled, a red mark across the bridge of his nose and saliva sliding down his chin. He slept fitfully.

But soon he awoke, and looked at us, and smiled. And then one of the most wonderful scenes I have ever witnessed took place. Carefully, lovingly, Mom handed Dad his dentures, which, in his vanity, he had never before been without. He fitted them into his mouth, and his face brightened. Almost ritualistically, she returned his glasses. His hearing aid. She dabbed his cheek and combed his hair. And at the last, she replaced his wedding ring on his finger.

Step by step she brought him back to her. Step by step he returned to her. Pure joy. Pure, sweet joy passing back and forth between them.

I stood nearby but, to them, not present. They were alone with each other.

I watched my elderly parents. Lovers. Still.

34. A Welcome Stranger

The best thing about the Bromley Mountain cafeteria is that you really can't distinguish an expert skier from a klutz. This serves me well. For all anyone knew, the telltale dampness along my right leg and buttock was a badge of honor won in a plucky but futile effort to better my record whizzing down a "ski at your own peril" slope. In fact, I had neglected to weight one foot while gliding along a nearly flat surface and took a modest tumble; fortunately, the two five-year-olds who had been headed in my direction deftly avoided my prone body.

But inside, who would know? The interior of the building was a melting pot, figuratively and literally. Amateur and skilled skiers blended together, indistinguishable save for the subject of their conversation. The rooms were warm. Hats and gloves and goggles and scarves were removed and jackets unzipped as tired upscale athletes inelegantly clomped across the wooden floors in their high plastic boots.

Ruddy-faced men and women, some with eyebrows still frosted, offered credit cards to the sallow cashier, and then, carefully balancing blue trays, marched off to join companions at their tables. Freezing-cold day. Cozy restaurant. Hot food. Perfect.

I passed through the cafeteria line, selecting items I would never otherwise consider, but rationalizing how on this nippy day of physical exertion my body needed — no, deserved — usually forbidden items. My skiing partner and I found spaces at a table near the center of the room, lifted our heavy legs over the benches, and sat down. Ahhh! That felt good.

Surrounding us was the usual cross-section of types, from parents lunching with infants borrowed from their day in the resort's nursery to members of the "Over 70 Club" who receive complimentary lift passes. Snow boarders (distinguished by their simple boots and bulky clothing), French Canadians (speaking animatedly in — what else — French), and perfectly coifed snow bunnies and snow hares all added to the friendly mix.

Among that crowd, a few tables over from mine, a father and two children sat eating their lunches. The girl was probably nine or ten, the boy about seven. There were spaces between them and the others sharing the long table; they seemed to be alone.

My skiing partner and I were in the midst of a discussion, halfway through our lunch, when I looked over his shoulder and noticed that some of the people nearby were staring in our direction. They were not smiling. I paused midsentence, and heard a single, loud voice coming from behind me, a couple of tables away. The father with his two children.

What I saw when I swiveled around was a very large man yelling at a very small boy. A turtleneck and a sweater and a puffy ski jacket added to his size. His face was now an angry crimson, not the glowing pink derived from sun and cold. The man was enraged, and his voice seemed to become even louder as other conversations halted. After a while he must have begun hearing himself, and quickly lowered his volume to a controlled, contemptuous monotone.

The little girl was busy. Busy looking at distant signs, distant objects, distant people, distant anything. She seemed to be engaged in a well-practiced routine.

And the little boy just stared at his food while his father raged on. The child grew smaller and smaller inside the bulk of his clothing, like a trapped spider folding its legs into itself, trying to disappear. No eye contact. No defense. No response. Not even tears.

The attack continued rapid-fire until the father felt a

hand on his shoulder. He was not being grabbed. Just a hand, resting gently. He looked up to see a stranger, a fellow perhaps fifteen years his senior, standing there, masking his anger, trying, rather, to appear bemused. "Hey, hey" he said quietly, "it's okay. You know, let's all just...enjoy the day."

The father's eyes shifted back and forth from the boy to the interloper. He seemed to take a deep breath, then motioned for the children to finish eating. At last, the attack had ended. The older man gracefully accepted the sneer he received, but as he turned away, his face changed from frozen neutrality to a mixture of disgust and sadness.

Later, outside near the lift line, I witnessed another brief encounter between the two men, this one less civil as the angry younger man taunted the older, demanding to know how *dare* he intervene in someone else's business, how *dare* he tell someone else what to do. They drew closer and closer, the diatribe punctuated by the father's frequent "Huh? Huh? Huh?" barroom brawl kind of challenge.

From my distance I couldn't hear all the words, but the confrontation ended as the older man declined to respond in kind to the abuse and seemed to say, gently, "Just be calm. I was concerned for the child. Just, you know, take it easy."

That marked the end of the encounter. A minidrama in two very brief acts. And now it was over. Except for one final detail.

Somewhere there is a seven-year-old boy who, short-changed in parenting, learned that his father's abuse is unacceptable and that someone else, someone he'd never seen before and will never see again, cared.

– XI –

From Fear to Faith

35. Choosing a Different Path

Years ago, during a beautiful autumn day in Vermont, our family joined with our friends the Campbells for a hike up the side of Equinox Mountain, the high peak that overlooks our little village. It was the height of foliage season, and the state was overrun with tourists and cyclists and cars idling while their drivers turned maps upside down and sideways.

We decided to retreat to the solitude of the now orange and yellow and red crest that protects our community from the evil that otherwise would creep across from neighboring New York.

Cameras and hiking sticks in hand, we walked up Prospect Street to the dirt road that becomes a path, circled around Equinox Pond and the old dance pavilion by its shore, and then forged into the woods, heading up the trail toward Deer Knoll.

It took us about an hour, perhaps an hour and a quarter, to reach our goal, a rocky ledge that sits halfway up this lovely mountain and offers its spectacular view of the valley.

We rested on the rocks, took pictures of each other, and drank in the beauty of our village below. And then it was time to descend.

I was a little bit concerned because we seemed to be heading in a different direction with little evidence of the route by which we had ascended.

But Orland Campbell, our friend and neighbor, and that day, our guide, explained to me why there was nothing to worry about: There are really two ways to go down the mountain; one way is by following the well-worn path, taking the familiar route.

But it is possible to select another way to return to the village. It involves simply descending at any point desired.

No matter where one wanders, as long as the flow of gravity is followed, one will ultimately reach the road.

This alternate way sometimes involves a sharper descent, a little bit of climbing downward, perhaps a fall or two as the terrain becomes steep and rocks and branches give way.

But it's an exhilarating way to descend. More challenging, of course. Less repetitious, more exciting and unpredictable.

That autumn day on the mountain we all chose to descend not by the traditional paths but rather by the alternate routes. Each created his or her own trail, and we all spent a happy half hour or so quickly bouncing down the mountain, sometimes out of sight but always reassuringly shouting back and forth to one another.

Ultimately we reached our goal, our homes in the valley. We were invigorated, energized. We had chosen what Robert Frost called the road "less taken, less traveled by."

It made a difference that day. It usually does.

36. The Rabbi/Stand-Up Comic

"Ski emergency."

That's the code we use to describe a cloudless Vermont day with temperatures hovering in the midtwenties and an uncrowded, snow-packed mountain beckoning seductively for us to cruise down its untrafficked runs. I alerted my friend Dick Ringenwald, minister of the local Congregational church, and could sense the despair in his reply. "Sorry," he said. "I've got to finish Sunday's sermon. I'm really boxed in here."

Five minutes passed. Then my phone rang. Dick. "Oh. Okay. Let's go."

Thirty minutes later we were on the lift, and thirty-seven minutes later we were zipping single file down the expert slope, which, under these perfect conditions, entices mediocre skiers like us into thinking we're pretty darn good. Dick's a better skier than I, but, fortunately, also older, so we are a fairly even match. Neither of us is competitive. He is the sole minister with many responsibilities to a large congregation, and I continually remind myself that a stand-up comic definitely needs to be able to stand up. And so we took our refreshing runs at a relaxed, safe pace, pausing to appreciate the magnificent views while the burning sensations in our thigh muscles receded.

After a few runs that morning Dick told me the theme of his sermon, and I supplied him with an opening joke. That bought him an extra half hour on the mountain, but finally he yielded to the siren call of the word processor awaiting him in his study. I continued to ski by myself.

The double chairlift was running at half capacity on this quiet Friday. No waiting. Still, I nodded to another apparently lone skier, and we agreed to ride up together.

It's a good way to pass the time, and, I always find, an opportunity to meet interesting people.

During the first minutes we predictably expressed mutual delight over the splendid weather and snow conditions as well as our good fortune in being able to have the mountain nearly to ourselves. Then, at about the halfway marker, following a slight pause in our conversation, the inevitable. Looking straight ahead, the sun glinting off his yellow goggles, he asked, "So, whadda you do?"

"I'm a rabbi and a stand-up comic."

Another pause. He pushed his goggles onto his forehead, turned to me with a vaguely skeptical smile, and said, "Really?"

Now, this is the moment I love. And I'm always prepared for it, even on a ski lift. I reached into my jacket pocket and presented him with my business card, which states, rather elegantly, I think,

Dr. Robert A. Alper
Rabbi/Stand-up Comic
(Really)

The stranger chuckled, then launched an effusive monologue. "A stand-up comic. You must be so brave! You know, I can't imagine anything more frightening than trying to make people laugh. To me, that's ultimate danger. That takes real courage."

I blushed beneath my goggles and accepted his accolades modestly. Then I attempted to steer the conversation in a different direction.

"How about you? What do you do?"

"Me?" he replied (and-I-am-not-making-this-up, as humorist Dave Barry often writes), "Oh, I'm a fireman in Bedford-Stuyvesant."

Now it was my turn to be incredulous. "You fight fires

in one of New York's most dangerous neighborhoods, and you think *I'm* brave?!"

He had as many questions for me as I had for him. I explained that when people hear of a rabbi who is a comedian, they assume that I'm a "humorist" or a "raconteur," who tells long, winding stories that end with a punch line dependent on a knowledge of Hebrew or Yiddish. Actually, I do pure stand-up, an act that was honed before typical comedy club audiences.

I pointed out some of the occupational hazards: hecklers, for example. I rarely encounter them, and when I do, I simply say, "Excuse me, sir, but would you mind leading us in the silent prayer?"

One time I finished a decent performance and left the stage to applause, feeling that wonderful "comedy high." As I passed through the middle of the room, a large fellow sprang to his feet, thrust out his hand, and said, "Bob! It's Barry Gordon! Great set!"

"Hi, Barry. Hey, thanks for coming. Glad you enjoyed it."

For the next twenty minutes I stood in the back and agonized. Who *is* this guy? Did I officiate at his wedding? Was he once a member of my congregation, or did I bury somebody in his family?

Finally — thankfully — it came to me. Three months earlier he had installed a nozzle on my furnace.

Our chair was approaching the summit of the mountain. It was my turn to ask the fireman how he could be so blasé about his occupation, and why he chose such a busy, dangerous place to work. "Simple," he responded. "I like to fight fires, and Bed-Sty is a neighborhood where there are lots of fires. I don't want to sit in a station house all day." He gave me a matter-of-fact smile, and we skied down the unloading ramp.

We zigged and zagged our way to the base of the mountain and by unspoken mutual consent paired up again on the lift. Each had lots to inquire of the other, and the questions were similar. We asked each other about danger, and concluded that lack of control was the scariest part of both professions.

A modest, laconic fellow, he briefly described one occasion when he was temporarily trapped in a fiery attic and another when his engine collided at high speed with a truck. My contribution to the topic: a memorable ladies' luncheon, early in my comedy career, when I was forced to perform following a dynamic speaker who made such an emotional speech that not only were the audience members sobbing audibly, but I, too, was sniffling, and even the busboy had tears rolling down his face. Then immediately back to the MC: "And now, friends, let's look at the lighter side of life with the comedy of Rabbi Bob Alper."

I would hardly equate the two kinds of "danger," but the fireman assured me that my experience was one he hoped never to face.

Before we parted, we agreed: Each person has different talents, different fears. I would never choose to enter a burning building. He would never attempt to make people laugh for ninety minutes. The beauty of the divine plan is that each person possesses unique abilities, and the most fortunate among us are those who can find ways to use those talents while somehow contributing to the betterment of humanity.

I often think about the encounter with the courageous Bedford-Stuyvesant fireman, and still chuckle at the thought that he thinks *I'm* brave. And certainly, I decided, there is no way I could ever seriously equate our two professions. Until I heard a story from a rabbi who approached me after I did a show for a large conference of Jewish educators.

I nurture a mental treasure trove of special compliments that have followed my performances. Every entertainer does; it's a healthy way to emotionally balance the occasionally negative remarks. For example, I will never forget the woman who explained, "Six months ago my husband died. Tonight is the first time I've laughed." And I cherish the image passed on to me by a grateful husband about the way he and his wife smile during her chemotherapy treatments while they listen to my audiotape through headsets.

But the rabbi's story left me breathless. She appeared in front of me and was gone in less than a minute. I think she may have been in a hurry. Or shy. Or perhaps she was telling me about herself. "A friend," she said, "is struggling with cancer. She's a young woman with little children, and it's been a very difficult battle. Sometimes the woman goes into suicidal depressions."

"Whenever that happens," my informant concluded, "she listens to your tape. It cheers her up, and then she is able to function again."

So maybe the fireman and I have more in common than I thought. Maybe we're both involved in rescue work, he actively, I in a more passive manner, with rescue a by-product of the laughter I provide. It's a terribly humbling, exciting thought, one that confirms the consistency between being a rabbi and being a stand-up comic. But I guess I've known all along that clean, unhurtful humor can be healing and therapeutic and health-giving.

In a way, we all do rescue work when, intentionally or unintentionally, we touch other people's lives in positive ways: the kind word, the unanticipated compliment, the sharing of a sweet memory, the unexpected favor, the helpful gesture, the empathetic grimace. That's how we — all of us — rescue one another. In little ways, day by day.

It's unusual, my dual career. No doubt about it. Interesting, too. People are fascinated to learn about it, whether from newspaper articles, on radio and television shows, or just one on one, sharing a lift chair on a perfect Vermont "ski emergency" kind of morning.

I'm a very lucky guy. The more I understand about this career and realize how smiles and laughter fit into the divine plan, the more I feel particularly blessed to be able to spend this part of my life as both a rabbi and a stand-up comic.

Really.

37. The Man Who Was "Not Religious"

Reverend Martin Luther King, Jr. had been assassinated a few months earlier.

Washington, D.C., had been engulfed in race riots marked by killing, looting, and burning.

Resurrection City, a tent encampment in the heart of the Capitol, had just been forcibly dismantled.

Now the National Guard patrolled the city, the smell of tear gas lingering everywhere and sickening even soldiers equipped with masks.

It was my first day on the job, a "Rabbinical Internship in Urban Affairs," July 1968.

The idea was to take student rabbis — there were four of us, all in our midtwenties, serving in different cities — and arrange for us to experience urban life close up, from inside, as much as possible. Those were heady times, probably because after the riots everyone thought things were so bad, they could only get better, and we would play a role in the reconstruction and healing.

I reported to a supervisor at the local Jewish Community Relations Council. He would point me in a direction and provide me with some background information, but it was largely up to me to define my role while learning as much as I could. During the first week I attended emergency meetings of the district government, met with people who studied the inner city, and listened to agency officials assess the ongoing crisis. High-profile stuff. Suits and ties. Superfluous.

Late that week, as I was driving through one of the most devastated parts of the district, the corner of Fourteenth

Street and Euclid Avenue, I noticed several pickets parading back and forth in front of a newly reopened store. The writing on the signs was small, and I was curious, so I parked my car and walked by the burned-out storefronts to a point where I could read the slogans. "No More Liquor Stores," they proclaimed. Prior to the riots, prior to the burning of all the stores for blocks around, the area had been flooded with liquor stores. Now, the first place to open for business again turned out to be a liquor store.

A few residents had launched a protest. Their leader was Robert King, an energetic twenty-eight-year-old African-American who lived nearby.

I spoke with King for a while, marching in step with him as he paced the oval route back and forth in front of the store. This was just the beginning, he told me. First, protest the liquor stores. Next, set up a day care center, and then a facility for food and clothing distribution. His friendliness was appealing, and his vision and energy complimented each other. I was impressed, and asked how I might help.

Well, he said, his volunteers need an office. That's the first thing. A local landlord offered to give King and his people temporary use of a destroyed pawnshop. Not a pretty sight, but it had a roof that didn't leak and a front door that could be locked. Problem was, the place was totally empty. If they were to accomplish anything, they needed at least some furniture. I said I'd see what I could do.

The next day I called a large synagogue and spoke with the rabbi, who gave me the name of one of his congregants, a man who owned a company that sold used office furniture. I've never been comfortable asking for donations, but since it was stranger to stranger over the telephone, I worked up the courage. I will never forget our conversation.

I introduced myself, explaining how I had been referred by the rabbi. Briefly I described what I was doing in Washington, outlined King's plans, and asked the man if there were some way he could help us obtain a few desks and chairs. I held my breath.

His answer was abrupt. "Sure. Come over and pick out what you need."

And just as quickly, he changed the subject. Told me how he really likes the rabbi at his congregation, how he's been a member for more years than he can recall, and concluded with a confession, "But you know, I don't attend services very often. I'm not religious."

"I'm not religious." A thirty-second request from a stranger and the man was willing to donate furniture to an unknown activist named Robert King and his yet-to-be-formed grass-roots effort to help the poor.

I was still mulling over his "confession" as I asked how we could get the furniture to the pawnshop.

"We'll deliver it. Just stop by, pick out what you need, and it'll be delivered the next day. Anyway, as I was saying, I support the synagogue but feel guilty about not attending as often as...."

Later in my career I would learn how to explain to people like the furniture man that in my view, they may not be ritualistic, but they are very religious, authentically religious, in the ways they humbly, eagerly, and very naturally do their part to create a better world. What I did say is, "On the basis of a call from a stranger you're willing to donate office furniture to a second stranger of a different race and a different religion and a different community solely on the claim that he's hoping to help people. I think you're a deeply religious person."

And a modest one, too. He really didn't want to hear what I was now saying, and politely ended the conversation.

The next day Robert King received his desks and chairs, and for the rest of the summer he and a few other volunteers worked in the sooty shell of a ruined pawn shop to lay the foundations of the Columbia Heights Community Association. I continued to lend a hand, then returned to the seminary in the fall. When I visited Robert in December, he had moved around the corner and occupied several large basement rooms in an apartment building. The place was bursting with clothing and food staples, a well-organized, efficient place of cheerful help in a neighborhood of sadness.

Thanks, in part, to a man who was "not religious."

– XII –

From Defeat to Defeat to Defeat . . . Until Victory

38. Transcending Murphy's Law

The .38 caliber snub-nose revolver pointed straight up in the sky, one or two inches from my right ear. That's regulation: Hold the gun securely, directed away from accidental targets whenever running with the weapon drawn.

And I was running.

The morning sun was shining brightly, but most of the time I found myself in the dark shadows beneath the bellies of a long row of railroad tank cars. The sheriff and I quickly developed a rhythm: Race past one car, then squat down next to the second, and scan the rusty tracks for any movement. Repeat the same maneuver.

The running was difficult. A dark suit and leather shoes isn't the best outfit for this kind of exercise, and neither the wooden ties nor the gravel bed beneath provided very secure footing. Still, we loped on ahead, panting, perspiring, until we reached the chain link fence marking the end of the yard.

The sheriff pointed to a section of the fence that had been folded back, providing an uncharted, suspicious exit. Still clutching our revolvers, we edged through the crease and scurried up an embankment that emptied out onto an old tar parking lot overgrown in most places with grass and weeds.

The lot looked abandoned, except for a single old yellow school bus eternally resting on six very flat tires. Now we walked toward the bus, cautiously, the sheriff scanning off to the left and I to the right. When we reached the rear door, the guns that had been pointing at the clouds were lowered and aimed. Legs spread for balance, I gripped my .38 with two hands while the sheriff opened the door and peered in.

As soon as his eyes adjusted to the dim light, he holstered

his gun and leaped up onto the bumper, then charged into the bus. At the front end, manacled to an old wooden chair, mouth taped shut, a beautiful woman desperately tried to telegraph with her eyes that any sudden motion would set off the bomb beneath her. The sheriff screamed for me to run around to the passenger door. I took three steps, turned left, and —

"Cut."

"Good one," the director said. "I think we got it. Mark, check the framing."

Another morning on the set of *Diamond Run,* an action-packed, full-length feature film shot in Manhattan and Vermont, and including in its cast a small, select role for one fifty-year-old guy who finally got to do what he dreamed about at age nine.

Graceful heroes, snarling villains, a gorgeous damsel in distress. The movie had everything, including the implosion of an eight-story building, helicopters, car crashes, and plenty of old-fashioned fisticuffs. I played the rather bumbling local FBI agent, and my most dramatic scene had me knocking — forcefully — on a motel room door. Of course I did get to drive a Mazda Miata convertible in one scene, but since I covered only about forty feet, my top speed reached a perky 25 mph.

So, Rabbi, how did you end up playing cops and robbers in a Rutland, Vermont, train yard?

Simple. I knew the right people at the right time and the right place. Plus, I had gray hair and was willing to work for free, enough of a combination to launch a cinematic career.

David Giancola, the director, and his partner, Peter Beckwith, formed a video company a few years back. They grew rapidly, branching out into "industrials" and cable TV, eventually producing a relatively low-budget feature film called *Time Chasers*. That movie's success led to a second effort, *Diamond Run,* a more substantial venture featuring a few Hollywood actors, a real stuntman, a host of camera operators, lighting people, prop handlers, a makeup artist, acting coaches, production assistants, caterers, and some local "talent," including yours truly.

Mine was a "bit part" with appearances in seven or eight scenes, the most exciting of which was that rail yard sequence. Typical of the rest of "my" scenes (and a full day's work) was one in which I walked into a room demanding, "Where's the girl?"

And cut.

About six weeks after the filming concluded, I stopped into Edgewood Video, just to say hello and see how things were progressing now that the editing stage had begun. I found David the director lounging on an old couch in what was the sheriff's office but now had returned to being a reception area. A mostly eaten Italian hoagie and an empty bag of potato chips were spread out on the coffee table, and he was finishing off a Pepsi.

"The rest of the shoot went very well," David told me, "with only one focus problem requiring a remake. And that could be done in Manhattan without the actors present." He flipped a cassette into a machine and showed me some of the action footage made on days when I was not on the set. I was amazed.

Even better news was the fact that based only on a synopsis and a few outtakes, the distributor had already sold the film in two foreign countries. David was obviously pleased. And relieved.

Which led me to a question I had considered all through the project. "What really impressed me," I said, "was that there you were, day after day single-handedly steering a huge investment, organizing a couple dozen people, contending with everything from trucks backfiring to small-fry like me who couldn't remember my lines, and you always seemed to have a smile, you always seemed relaxed, even to the point of actually enjoying yourself. How could you do that?"

David grinned, shyly this time, and then shared with me a bit of philosophy that he claims is almost a film-industry standard, but, I suspect, is also very much a natural function of the kind of person he is.

"First of all," he began, "directing a film is what I live for, what I love doing. No matter how difficult a scene might be, I constantly remind myself, 'David! You're really doing it! You're actually directing a feature film!'

"And when you direct a film," he continued, "everything is on the line. All the long-range planning, the preparation, the raising of investment money, the dreaming — everything comes down to those critical moments between 'Action' and 'Cut.' Often there are dozens of people contributing to each shot, from the actors to the technical people to the dialogue coaches and prop handlers. Everybody looks at me. I set the tone. If I seem nervous, the whole enterprise becomes tense, and the product suffers. But if I seem relaxed, the cast and crew relaxes, too, and then they can pour their energies into their work. It's far easier for magic to happen when we're all enjoying ourselves."

So David smiled a lot on set. It was indeed infectious. And a very effective way to run part of a business.

There was more. David told me that the school bus scene was originally to have been shot in a railroad passenger car, but somebody neglected to notify someone else, and then the train was unavailable. The school bus provided an adequate last-minute substitute, but the filming schedule had to be reconfigured since the bus was due back in service almost immediately.

"That's how it is, making a film. There's a certain absolute: Things over which you have no control *will* go wrong," David observed. "You have to expect it, and you can't let it get you. You have to be able to adapt, to improvise, to change plans quickly and go right on, even with a smile. Otherwise, you get bogged down and defeated by the glitches, and the whole project suffers."

"Things over which you have no control *will* go wrong. You have to expect it." I wish I'd been more aware of David's philosophy that day in March 1993, as I changed planes in Pittsburgh en route to perform stand-up comedy for five hundred people in Minneapolis. Just as the passengers were about to board, the announcement rang through the building, "Due to the severity of the blizzard, the airport will be closed until tomorrow morning at the earliest."

"Things *will* go wrong." I accepted the cancellation with resignation but not grace. Somehow I caught the last bus out of the airport before even the roads were closed, and I made it to a large downtown hotel where I ended up spending two days and nights in the middle of a major dance competition. The place was bursting with seven hundred ten-year-olds and their mothers in sequins, tutus, and enough hairspray to power the plane home.

Now I can laugh. I should have laughed more back then, too. David is right.

Late some evening when you're fighting insomnia and switching through the channels, if you come across a scene of two grim-faced guys racing — or, well...moving determinedly — through a line of railroad tank cars, be aware that the older fellow in the gray suit is me. I may look serious, but underneath I was having the time of my life.

And just a few yards away, right next to the camera, the director was grinning.

39. Gerda's Gift

It was while flying into Memphis, of all places, that the number began making just a little more sense.

My preference is to sit toward the front of an airplane, on the aisle, bulkhead if possible. That way I can exit faster, without spending five long minutes scrunched beneath the overhead rack while Mr. and Mrs. Just-Back-from-Palm-Beach slowly gather their shopping bags and straw hats.

This plane was only half full, and since I'd never been to Memphis, I moved over to the window for a look at the city as we circled before landing.

I do a lot of thinking on planes. For one thing, despite statistics that show flying is a very safe form of travel, buzzing along at 33,000 feet in a metal cigar often evokes in me an involuntary confrontation with mortality. One deep and serious thought leads to another, and that's where the number came up once again.

Memphis, this flat sprawl of river and skyscrapers and surrounding suburbs, serves a population of just over one million. One million, seven thousand and three hundred, according to the AAA guidebook. One million people. One million people's offices and schools and stores and hospitals and homes and factories and trains and roads and cars and churches and synagogues and parks and theaters and more. One million people. It's really impossible to try to comprehend such an enormous number.

And then the thought occurred to me:

Times six.

One million people. Times six. Six million. The number of Jews murdered by the Nazis and their accomplices during the Holocaust.

Six times the population of greater Memphis. Enough

men, women, and children to inhabit all I could see from the window of the 737. Six times over.

I can't comprehend the number.

Other attempts are equally unsuccessful. A football game in Rich Stadium south of Buffalo: eighty thousand cheering people. A lull in the game and I look around, look at all the different faces close by, at the blur of bright winter clothing way across the field. And with a little math I begin to think: six million people. That would include every single person sitting in this stadium — times seventy-five.

I can't comprehend the number. But I keep trying. In one way or another, throughout my life, I've tried to understand the Holocaust. In the course of my rabbinate I've never been much interested in preaching my "absolute truth" about the nature of God, or dictating a description of some kind of afterlife or the requirements that one must fulfill to be a good Jew. Maybe it would have been different had I been born to a later or even earlier generation. But now, for me, trying to understand my people's recent catastrophe, trying to find some sense, some sense at all, has overwhelmed and channeled my most serious spiritual thoughts.

Even while watching out an airplane window as it slowly descends toward greater Memphis, population 1,003,700.

Especially helpful along the way has been the privilege of knowing one particular woman who has become the most important of all my teachers.

The tenth-grade Confirmation class at Buffalo's Temple Beth Zion met every Monday evening. A newly minted assistant rabbi, I taught one fifteen-kid section while the senior rabbi, the cantor, and the principal taught the other sections. Once a month we'd all dine on pizza and Cokes and hear a speaker or watch a relevant movie.

The speaker scheduled for the first Monday in November happened to be the mother of Jimmy Klein, one of the kids in the class. I asked my colleagues about her topic and was told that she'd be speaking about her life. In fact, she had written an autobiography called *All But My Life*. Her name was Gerda Klein.

The book chronicled Gerda's years as a teenager through her early twenties, years that saw a warm and sweet family life transformed into a seemingly endless Holocaust nightmare: the disappearance and death of her family, slave labor, unspeakable deprivation, and, finally, survival, rescue, and a new life in the United States.

Sometimes when I am reading a book, a word or a phrase will suddenly leap out at me and grab my attention in unanticipated ways. That's what happened with *All But My Life*. I'm not sure, but I think Gerda cited only one or two dates throughout the entire book. In the midst of hell, dates have no purpose; the only mileposts are the cold, the heat, the snow, the mud.

Still, for some reason, Gerda did refer to one particular date. It was the day on which she and 2,000 other young Jewish women began a forced march from which a mere 120 would ultimately survive three months later. The date was January 29, 1945.

January 29, 1945. On the very same wintry day when two thousand Jewish teenage girls were being kicked and beaten along a desolate road, most heading ultimately toward their deaths, another much more conventional drama was taking place in a cozy hospital thousands of miles to the west.

Providence, Rhode Island. January 29, 1945. The day I was born.

So that's what was happening when I made my debut. In Providence, a baby boy was born. Celebration. Thanksgiving. Phone calls up and down the East Coast, and warm good wishes to my parents and grandparents. Thousands of miles away, in Grünberg, Germany, two thousand Jewish girls began a bitterly cold three-month death march accompanied by shouts and whips and rifles.

In a soft, soothing voice Gerda told the Confirmation class her story. The fifteen and sixteen-year-olds heard about other Jewish teenagers who experienced a hellish world not so long before. It was a story they would never forget.

Since that introduction I've heard Gerda speak innumerable times, not only to Confirmation classes but also to adult groups and even on the Emmy- and Oscar-winning HBO documentary about her life. And each time I learn something new. Each time Gerda includes a gently powerful lesson that enhances my life, that blesses my life.

I especially remember a brief story Gerda told to one of the Confirmation classes. A crisp Buffalo winter evening. The kids, teachers, and a few helping parents lounged around long tables covered with empty salad bowls, some half-eaten pizzas, and a collection of soda cans. A few announcements, an introduction, and Gerda began to speak.

As always, Gerda related her experiences in quiet, gentle tones, straightforward, matter-of-fact, almost hypnotic. Only after listening to Gerda many times can one disengage ever so slightly enough to realize what an eloquent speaker she is, and how her very plain words are infused with philosophy, theology, and life-directing guidance worthy of the wisest counselor.

One learns from what Gerda says, and one learns equally from what Gerda does not say. There is no bitterness or hatred or vengeance. Only her story and an affirmation of life.

This is what she taught me one night.

Gerda shared an account of her Holocaust experience, including the way her friend Ilse Kleinzahler, just before she died in a cold, drizzly field in Czechoslovakia, made Gerda agree to the impossible: that she would try to live one more week. Gerda promised, and in exactly one week, she was liberated.

Fifteen or so years later Gerda was living in Buffalo, a wife, a mother with two elementary school daughters and the youngest child, Jimmy, in kindergarten. Today was Jimmy's turn: It was his assembly, a play or recital of some sort, the kind in which each serious little child speaks a word or two as cameras click and families smile broadly but try not to giggle or laugh.

A lull in the presentation and a neighbor turned around in her seat to see Gerda. "What are you doing here?" she asked. "I thought you were speaking in Pittsburgh last night."

"I did," Gerda responded.

"Then how did you get here?"

"By bus."

By bus. There were no late evening or early morning flights, so Gerda took a bus through the night in order to be present for Jimmy's kindergarten performance.

She took a bus because, she knew, deep in her heart, that Ilse would have given everything, everything, to be able to do what Gerda did. Ilse would have crawled from Pittsburgh to Buffalo to see her little boy standing there on the stage.

"Ilse would have crawled from Pittsburgh to Buffalo...."
More than two decades later, I can still hear Gerda's matter-of-fact statement. Not self-righteous. Not preachy. To Gerda, it was a simple, understandable conclusion. Logical.

But to me, those words form part of a spiritual beacon that emanates from the Holocaust and has illuminated my life in profoundly positive ways. Since I first heard

Gerda recount that story, I never again attended one of my kids' presentations without thinking, Ilse would have crawled....And I never again attended one of my kids' presentations without thinking, *This moment is holy.*

I can't comprehend the number six million. And by the same token, I can't fathom the extraordinarily large number of people who participated in the murders and then blithely went on with their lives. I can't grasp the numbers, but looking toward Rwanda and Bosnia, for example, I can indeed believe that evil is real, and that ordinary people can commit monstrous acts, even in this modern age.

The enormity of evil in my lifetime makes it extremely difficult for me to comprehend a God who is both omnipotent and benevolent. A person emerges from a building collapse and credits God for the "miracle" of his survival. And I wonder: What about the other people, the people who did not survive? Why no miracle for them? I can't imagine a God who would pick and choose in that way. For one to imply that God saved him or her while allowing others to die is at best naiveté, at worst, theological arrogance.

What, then, can we understand about evil? Only that it exists not as isolated events but in vast, unfathomable quantity. In the solitude of an airplane, watching a city of one million come into view as we descended below the clouds, another thought occurred to me. To destroy, to liquidate, to kill, this many children, and women, and men — what a monumental number of people it would take to carry out that grim task.

And two generations ago it actually happened. Times six. The mind cannot really comprehend. The very thought crushes the spirit.

But then I visualize Gerda once again, standing before sixty teenagers whose secure world she never knew, and

I think of the message she imparted to them after she guided them through her years of fear and deprivation and horrendous loss.

The typical teenage chattiness and giggling and posturing had ended moments into Gerda's presentation. They sat at those same dining tables, now silent, sad, dazed by the world to which they had been exposed, knowing that from this point forward their lives would never quite be the same. How to internalize what they had learned about the nature of mundane evil, about the vulnerability of Jews? How to comprehend the fate they had evaded by the lucky accidents of geography and a handful of decades?

Gerda understood their struggle. She might have parted from them with a final warning. An admonition. A challenge. Instead, she gave them a gift.

All along that death march, Gerda gently related, the ragged, starving girls passed by homes with lights in the windows and smoke rising from the chimneys against the frosty nights. "That was my dream. My fantasy. That is what I longed for. Not riches or fame or possessions. Just a home. My home. What I wanted more than anything else in the world was the chance to go home, to sit in my living room while my father smoked his pipe, my mother crocheted little roses on sweaters, and my brother Arthur did his homework. That's what I yearned for more than anything else imaginable.

"So allow me to ask you to do one simple thing," Gerda concluded. "When you return to your homes tonight, don't enter right away. Just pause for a moment, and look at your house. Think about its warmth, its security. And think about the people inside, your family. Think about what they really mean to you, and what blessings you possess."

I suppose I'll always try to conceptualize that number six million. I'll continue to play grim mathematical games in airplanes, in stadiums, all with a similar result: The number six million is simply unfathomable.

But...I'll remember always the story of one family, of one young woman, and the life she fashioned after she emerged from the horror. Gerda's words are as clear to me today as they were when I first heard them, probably because I think of them so often. My home. My family. My blessings. I pause often as I enter my home, remembering Gerda, remembering what life was for some, what life still is for others. I think of Gerda often. She taught me how and why to love life in ways no others have. She honored me with a precious gift.

I share it gladly.

40. Fraternal Recognition

Where I live, Vermont, the weather can get pretty nippy. We like the cold, especially on bright, sunny winter days. I suppose that local TV meteorologists would keep us thoroughly informed about temperatures and especially wind-chill factors if we had local TV meteorologists, which we don't. We don't even have local TV.

There are basically three kinds of winter discussions. "Gettin' cold" (coats begin to replace sweaters and light jackets); "Real cold out there" (add hats and gloves, though I can rarely find mine the first time I need them); and "Dueling temperatures" in which townspeople try to one-up each other. "Hit eighteen below at my house this morning." "We're up on Danby Mountain Road. Dog woke me at four-thirty, and it was twenty-one below." Cold weather builds a community of ruddy-face people proud of their ability to cope with nature's extremes.

Deprived of pontification by computer-equipped forecasters, we pay little attention to concepts such as "wind chill factors." All we know is that if the thermometer says it's cold and the wind is blowing, people walk quickly from the car to the market, and business thrives at the full-service gas station in town.

My first significant encounter with "wind chill" took place, oddly enough, not in the dead of winter but on a Wednesday morning in July. At 6:45 A.M., to be specific. The thermometer offered a pleasant fifty-one degrees with the promise of a comfortably warm, dry day ahead. Cautiously overdressed in jeans, a shirt, a sweater, and my spring jacket, I hopped on my Yamaha Riva motor scooter, cranked up the engine, and headed to Rutland, thirty miles north, for an 8:00 A.M. motorcycle operator's test.

The scooter was a twenty-fifth anniversary present from my wife. It replaced the moped with which she had surprised me ten years earlier. That little thing, sort of a bicycle with a lawn-mower engine, couldn't make it up our steep hill and was gathering dust in the back of the garage. The Riva is big time, at least to me. It has a 200cc engine, whatever that means, a battery-operated starter, and enough power to fly up our bumpy, rutted hill if anyone is reckless enough to try.

Compared to the moped the scooter is a monster, a throbbing, powerful machine with a top speed I'll never experience. The first time out, as I cruised along at forty-five miles per hour, I began to think, *Hey! I'm a biker!* Then the first real motorcycle passed me, and I snapped back to reality. I recalled the story of the Jewish woman whose son bought a large boat. "By his wife," she said, "he's a captain. By his daughter and son, he's a captain. But by a captain . . . he's no captain." And, I suppose, I am no biker.

The difference between a motorcycle and my motor scooter? Well, if the theme song for a Harley-Davidson Fat Boy is "Born to Be Wild," the theme song for my Yamaha Riva is "Zippity Doo-Dah." It's that kind of vehicle. But I like it.

A driver's license suffices for a moped, but the scooter required a special permit and a road test. I achieved highest honors on the written exam, fifteen out of fifteen, and received a yellow form that allowed me to ride for two months during the day, without passengers. After a few weeks I made an appointment for the road test, and headed out that July morning. The morning I discovered the real meaning of wind chill.

I froze.

The first part of the trip took me along the side of the mountain on a dirt road, past the sheep farm and through the state forest. I rode slowly, cautiously, enjoying the misty morning scenery and the fresh, interesting scents that surprised me as I rounded each curve. It was 7:00 A.M. when I reached the two-lane blacktop. Now I was out in the open, part of a northerly flow of occasional traffic in which I was forced to pick up speed: forty, forty-five, sometimes fifty miles per hour. The faster I went, the chillier it became. Should I turn back for warmer clothing? It was all in the math: fifty-three, maybe fifty-five degrees. A forty-five-mile-per-hour wind hitting me square in the chest. And fifty minutes till my appointment some twenty-five miles away. I gritted my teeth and continued north.

When I gratefully dismounted at the Department of Motor Vehicles testing station, I discovered that I could not stop shaking. My upper body felt like a washing machine on a rocky spin cycle, wracked by uncontrollable internal aerobics. The dozen or so other examinees passed the time admiring one another's bikes and commenting on what a warm, lovely day it was.

After we registered in an office, the examiner told us to line up all of our motorcycles (and one scooter) at the edge of a course constructed of yellow lines on asphalt and some strategically placed orange cones. Each of us would be required to maneuver between the cones at slow speed, start and stop at designated points, and make a few sharp turns.

A teenage boy aced the course. A woman in her twenties, her boyfriend cheering her on, did reasonably well. And then it was the turn of the guy on the scooter, the guy who was at least two decades older than anybody else in the group.

Here's why I failed: I couldn't stop trembling. It's nearly impossible to finesse slow, delicate turns when your entire body is vibrating. To their credit, none of the others laughed, and the man from the Department of Motor Vehicles was particularly kind. After I knocked over all the cones, he told me, in a low voice, "Well, you lost some points here, but if you complete the rest of the course perfectly, you can still pass." I couldn't, and didn't.

The trip home was warmer. The sun had crested the eastern mountains, and the heat that now rose from the asphalt compensated for whatever wind chill remained. My body felt relaxed, soothed. My ego did not.

There was no rush to get home. No incentive, either. "Guess what? I failed my test. Couldn't steer a motor scooter between a few traffic cones." I bought gas in Wallingford, and stopped for coffee at Charlie's General Store in South Wallingford.

I tried not to dwell on the heavily philosophical aspects of the morning's washout, but I was feeling depressed about what had happened. This was not devastation, not a catastrophe. More of an annoying inconvenience than anything else, but with an obvious, and much more important subtheme of confrontation with my aging body and my mortality.

On the next leg, approaching the village of Danby, there's a fairly long, straight stretch of highway. I spotted him perhaps three-quarters of a mile in the distance, riding toward me on his shiny scarlet motorcycle. A real motorcycle, probably a Harley or a big Yamaha. We would pass by each other in a few seconds. "Born To Be Wild" meets "Zippity Doo-Dah," I thought ruefully. Not even "Zippity Doo-Dah." I was "Zippity Doo-Dah who couldn't pass a simple road test."

I stared straight ahead, thankful that my helmet and visor would obscure my dour expression. The person on the motorcycle was hunkered down, surging along the road in a smooth roar. Beneath the leather clothes, the visor, helmet, and gloves, it was impossible to determine whether the rider was a tattooed Hell's Angel or a vacationing accountant from New Jersey.

I would learn nothing else about him during the few seconds that elapsed as we drew closer. Except for one quality. He was charitable. I could tell by something he did with his left hand.

Ours was an inevitably brief encounter, riding in opposite directions at sixty and forty-five miles per hour. I never did see his face. He didn't turn his head in my direction. But just before we passed each other, in what surely took less than a second, the motorcyclist uncurled and straightened the middle, ring, and pinkie fingers of his left hand while maintaining his grip on the handlebar with his thumb and index finger. It was just a quick little motion. Recognition. Acknowledgment. A fraternal salute.

Biker to biker.

He probably saw my return wave. But I'm certain he couldn't hear my sudden burst of laughter above the sound of the engines.

Well, well. What do you know? Maybe I'm a biker after all, despite my failure!

The following summer I renewed my permit but didn't bother to travel up to Rutland for another road test. Sixty days' riding in summer daylight is plenty for me. Besides, the biggest thrill I get from using my motor scooter comes from cruising around town and chatting with people along the way. I ride slowly, only venturing out on warm, sunny days.

And whenever I see a two-wheeled vehicle approaching from the opposite direction, whether it's a thundering motorcycle, a motor scooter, or even a lowly moped, I offer one of those three-finger signals.

It's the biker way.

– XIII –

Life Is a Journey

41. Departures

When I was a smart young rabbi and knew quite a lot, I created worship services for little children, adapted baby-naming ceremonies, and lectured to new mommies and daddies about how to raise their children Jewishly.

Now I'm a not-as-smart middle-aged rabbi who wishes that somewhere, a more enthusiastic middle-aged colleague would create a life-cycle ceremony that addresses events I find myself going through: kids leaving home.

Sometimes it feels as if Judaism, and probably most other organized religions, guide and nurture us through the many stages of parenting, from birth rituals and the beginnings of religious education right on through the agony of adolescence. But suddenly it seems as if we parents are on our own at the parting, the moment when our children embark on the step that, for most, changes their status in our homes from resident to visitor.

Whether it's college, a job, the armed services, there comes that moment, and for parents the experience is often similar.

When I went off to Lehigh University in the fall of 1962, my parents drove me to campus, six hours from home. We unloaded my stuff, made the uncomfortable introductions with my roommates and the fearsome dorm counselor, and then my parents gracefully took their leave. About three decades later my mother confessed that after they exited the campus they pulled the car over to the side of the street, turned off the engine, and cried.

On a whitewater rafting trip in Idaho I became friendly with a fellow from Oregon named Patrick Michael Sean O'Halloran. He told me that when he entered college in 1961 his Irish Catholic parents drove him to the California campus. They unloaded the car quickly, and he was pleased that they departed soon after. A few miles into the trip home, Pat only recently learned, his parents pulled into a highway rest area, turned off the engine, and cried.

There must be a better way to launch children into their independence.

Some of life's major events are marked by a very discernible occurrence, the instant of birth being the most clear. Other events are spread out over time: the transition from babyhood to personhood, for example, or the passage through adolescence, which for some takes an entire decade. Even a wedding, though it has its prime moment, is diffused over the months of preparation and the hours of ceremonial festivities.

But that leave-taking comes upon us abruptly, sometimes with no forethought or preparation, and certainly without ritual to help us endure. It may happen in this way because our children are focused on what lies ahead, and we parents are equally invested in avoiding thinking about what their loss — and that is the key word — what their loss will mean to us, to our home, to our relationships. And so we all conspire to avoid thinking about what is about to happen.

I remember how our son left home.

Zack's departure was more complex than the norm. Our family was in a state of very happy transition, about to realize a long-held "impossible" dream of leaving our Philadelphia suburb and moving to Vermont. It was the end of June, and Sherri had already gone north to start her new job. Jessie had begun her final year at summer camp. Zack and I remained at the house.

I packed, while Zack celebrated his graduation from high school with a round of farewell parties. His plan was to spend the summer working at the New Jersey shore, living in a two-bedroom flat with a group of between three and eight other kids. At the end of August he would continue on to college in North Carolina.

At that time Zack was driving a 1984 Volvo sedan. I bought it new, thinking that it was the kind of car that I could use, then pass on to Sherri, and later, perhaps, even to the kids. At 124,000 miles it came into Zack's possession, and on that June day it was packed to the ceiling with all that was important to its owner.

"Gotta split, Dad. Josh is waiting at his house, and we're going to drive down to the shore together. Bye."

"Bye." Is that how childhood ends? "Bye?" Just like that?

As I headed out to the driveway, I started to think of a stroll I'd taken eighteen years earlier, down a hospital corridor that connected the delivery room with the nursery. Beside me a nurse guided a bassinet that contained a brandnew person. And the novel thought kept racing through my mind, I'm taking a walk with my son. With my son!

The screen door slammed behind me, a needed shock to my system that reminded me to stop being so damn lugubrious. After all, Zack was about to grab his independence. We raised him in that direction. He's just doing his job of separating, and he's doing it well. And besides, I would visit him at the shore in a few weeks.

But still... But still...

I walked over to the car. Looked it over, inspected the tires, and rearranged a piece of clothing that had gotten stuck in the door.

"Really, Dad. I've gotta go. Josh is waiting."

We gave each other a hug and a kiss. One of us had tears in his eyes and even down his cheeks, while the other gently broke away, started the car, and backed out of the driveway.

Zack paused in the road to shift gears. Then he slowly drove to the foot of our hill, toward the intersection where he would turn right and disappear from sight. I stood alone, watching as he edged away. A blurry maroon object growing smaller and smaller. A car, and my son, leaving his childhood home. Leaving his childhood. Forever.

And then my vision cleared slightly. I noticed that the old car's tailpipe was loose, sort of hanging by one clip. The forward thrust of the car made it flutter up and down, so gently, almost in slow motion.

It was phallic.

And it was waving to me.

That was probably the most highly charged, symbol-laden experience of my life, and I still have no idea exactly what the symbolism meant.

But I remember that wave.

– ❖ –

Four years later and it was Jessie's turn. By now the old Volvo had been handed to the youngest Alper, and with 187,000 miles on the odometer it was about to head toward another college. Jessie had blossomed into a free-thinking, independent, self-assured young woman, and since I could not guard or protect her any longer, I channeled some of my paternal caring into her car. At least I could feel useful during the countdown days before she, too, drove away.

They say history repeats itself. Ecclesiastes reminds us that there's nothing new under the sun. Yup.

Before it could pass the Vermont State inspection and the more stringent Robert Alper inspection, the Volvo needed the following: four new tires; rear brakes; shocks; struts; one headlamp; a rear muffler.

And a tailpipe.

A few weeks later a caravan comprised of two cars, two parents, one freshwoman, and one dog named Gideon drove the two-and-a-half hours south to Jessie's new college. A sensitively prepared schedule suggested we arrive around noon, help our child settle in, and join the president, faculty, and freshman class for a late-afternoon reception. Then we were equally sensitively urged to LEAVE. Which we did.

By 6:30 we found ourselves on the Taconic Parkway heading north. One empty car, two parents, and a dog. No radio. No conversation.

A few minutes into the trip a wave of righteous canine indignation overcame the dog when he realized that someone was occupying his seat next to the driver, his beloved master. Giddy was insistent, and Sherri in no mood to argue. She spent the entire trip home with a fifty-five-pound dog sitting in her lap. It provided needed diversion.

Later that night, after the answering machine was tended and the mail sorted, after the car was cleaned out and the throw rug Jessie decided she really didn't need was wrapped and placed in the cellar, I walked into her room and sat alone on the bench next to her picnic-table desk. The room had a sudden neatness about it that I knew I'd hate. I looked around at the hat collection, the posters on the walls, the rejected CDs and the high school notebooks strewn across the closet shelf.

I thought about the events of the day, thought how happy I was for her, and how proud. And also how sad, how selfishly sad I felt at her departure.

Sherri called out to find me, then came up to Jessie's room where she quietly joined me on the bench. We sat in silence for a while, just looking around.

42. Taking Yourself Lightly

During my first two years at the rabbinical seminary I taught at a local synagogue's religious school. Four of us car-pooled each Sunday.

Our group included a fellow named Arnie who is now a well-known and beloved West Coast spiritual leader; Herb, who earned his Ph.D. and now heads one of New England's largest, most prestigious congregations; David, who immigrated to Israel and coordinates a major international youth program; and yours truly, who immodestly thinks he's no slouch.

But back then ... well, we were four guys in a car pool. A boring car pool, until the day we pulled up to the Ludlow Avenue intersection just as the light turned red. Someone yelled, "Fire drill!" and as if part of the most graceful ballet, four doors flew open and four future rabbis sprang from the car and began circling the vehicle in a well-timed trot.

Someone shouted "Reverse," and, in perfect synch, each of us did a neat half turn and continued the trot, this time counterclockwise.

Nearby motorists looked puzzled, then amused, and finally rather impressed as we managed to leap into the car, slam the doors, and lurch forward at the very moment the light turned green.

Twenty minutes later I walked into my classroom to discover some two dozen mildly unruly sixth graders.

I told them to act their age.

– ❖ –

Those were interesting days at Hebrew Union College. Guys (and one woman) in our twenties, still young but preparing ourselves for careers that would depend on maturity and wisdom. One fellow was obviously a devotee of the old school of rabbinical affectation: He would practice walking up and down the sidewalk stooped over, as if concentrating on a heavy textual problem in the book he held. He dropped out of school in his second year.

But most of us persevered and ultimately became rabbis. And along the way, probably the best single piece of advice I ever heard was, "Don't take yourself too seriously. Take your work seriously, but take yourself lightly."

It makes good sense. And I never saw a better example than I did one late December day when I spent some time with Herb of "Fire Drill" fame at his New Haven synagogue.

Shortly after Hurricane Andrew devastated Florida, Herb decided to organize a benefit to aid in the rebuilding effort. With cosponsors from the community, Herb put together a comedy night at his synagogue. I was happy to volunteer my services, and the event raised more than $5,000, sent directly to relief agencies.

But it is not the fund-raiser that caught my attention that night. Collecting money to help others is a tradition. Good, decent people like Herb do it all the time.

Something else happened that night, something above and beyond happened that inspired me and made me smile.

Herb and I met at the synagogue on the afternoon of the performance. He gave me a tour: a beautiful sanctuary, magnificent facilities, and a huge, tastefully appointed rabbi's study, an appropriate office for the spiritual leader of such a prestigious institution.

I was impressed.

We spent an hour testing the sound system, adjusting the lights, and, along with Herb's six-year-old son, shooting nerf arrows around the auditorium.

I went back to my hotel to dress and have dinner with some other local friends.

That evening I drove back to the synagogue and parked in the lot. As I walked to the building, I saw a large van in the center of the drive just opposite the entrance doors. The driver was assisting eight or ten elderly people into the building.

As I drew closer, I was startled to realize that the driver was...Herb. A big smile on his face, he gently helped his charges negotiate the step and steadied them as they got their bearings on the pavement.

A few minutes later, after he parked the van, we spoke in his study. "What was that all about?" I asked.

"Oh," Herb replied in his wry, self-deprecating way, "we have a van for some of our elderly members. Since this is a holiday weekend, we couldn't get anyone to drive it. I didn't want them to miss out on your show."

So Herb drove the van. The distinguished rabbi of an eight-hundred-family congregation became a chauffeur for an evening, shuttling elderly men and women back and forth to a night of comedy.

To Herb this was no big deal. This is just part of what he does. This is who he is. But I saw a powerful message in action. Here was a man who doesn't take himself too seriously, but quite obviously takes very seriously his work as a rabbi. And because of that delicious combination of who he is, and what kind of rabbi he is, hurricane victims received help and a group of octogenarians spent a delightful evening laughing.

"Don't take yourself too seriously. Take your work seriously, but take yourself lightly."

43. Reincarnating (Sort of) the Dead

During the long New England winters, I was once told, certain Vermont entrepreneurs drive their trucks down to places like Hartford where they load up on used furniture and all kinds of bric-a-brac. Come summertime, they pitch a tent in a meadow near a rustic barn and hold old-fashioned auctions where eager tourists, nostalgic for the pleasures of the simple country life, bid high on rocking chairs and dressers and encrusted old tools. Then the visitors cart their booty back to their homes. In Hartford.

Frankly I see this as a grass-roots recycling program in which everybody wins. The Hartford dealers sell their wares, the auctioneers make a tidy profit, and the tourists depart our state bearing useful, tangible reminders of their idyllic days among the Green Mountains.

I've been doing pretty much the same thing, on and off, for about twenty years, only instead of auctioning furniture, I rescue old wooden windows, clean the frames, replace the glass with fresh mirrors, and sell them through a few local stores on consignment. The enterprise is part hobby, part small business. And in a larger sense, it's part recycling, part therapy.

Window mirrors. I didn't invent them, but I do accept credit for having imported the idea across the border many years ago after finding one in a Toronto shop. I was intrigued by what I saw: a simple rectangular sash whose crisp mirror panes, three over three, reflected the weathered wood surrounding them. I loved the contrast of new mirror and old wood together in one attractive wall hanging. And it just so happened that when we moved into our home in Buffalo in 1974, we inherited a few ancient window sashes that a previous owner forgot to toss out when replacing them with aluminum combinations.

And so began my new pastime, a pleasurable, somewhat creative activity with a spiritual content I never anticipated. I set out to have some fun with discarded window frames. The much loftier element of this work, resurrection, did not occur to me until much later.

Making window mirrors demands no artistry and not much craft. It's really only labor, usually enjoyable, with a bit of imagination and good luck needed at the outset. Yet the finished product is unique, beautiful. A lovely decoration for some, a new heirloom for others. Each step in the production provides a special benefit to the worker.

Finding the "raw material" can be the most challenging, the most fun. The frame in that Toronto shop was lovely, but also pedestrian. I decided to set my sights on anything except a square or a rectangle, the most common-type window. I searched for arches and circles and diamond shapes, curved tops and Gothic points and other distinct patterns. I discovered them in unusual places.

The most fascinating find was a set of squat four-foot-by-four-foot church windows with pointed tops and a wood circle in the interior. Ten or twelve of these frames, paint peeling away and glass shattered, had apparently sat for decades collecting pigeon droppings in the upper loft of an antiques dealer's barn outside Lititz, Pennsylvania, Amish country. The elderly proprietor merely pointed to their location. He was too frail to climb up. He and I negotiated a price of fifteen dollars each, and I can still see the "can-you-believe-it-I'm-actually-selling-those-useless-things" wink he gave his wife after we concluded the deal.

I loaded them into my utility trailer and hauled the treasure home. They turned out to be among the most stunning mirrors I ever made.

I found other frames buried under three feet of snow behind a closed factory in Phillipsburg, New Jersey; deep in the bowels of an unlighted, crowded storage trailer somewhere in Berks County, Pennsylvania; hidden among thousands of wooden shutters in a salvage lot; just sitting on the side of a suburban street, next to plastic bags bursting with other garbage awaiting the trash collector; and in a corner of Woodstock, Vermont's St. James Episcopal's rummage sale, where I bought one five-foot and one two-foot Gothic window frame, relics from a former church building that had been torn down at the turn of the century. Somebody had finally decided to clean out the cellar.

In virtually every one of these search-and-purchase transactions both the seller and the buyer secretly rejoiced in their good fortune. Seller: "It's a dream. I'm getting paid for this junk." Me: "Incredible. I've stumbled on another treasure." A nice way to do business.

The process of actually making the window mirrors involves several steps, and the first is by far the most fun. Virtually all of the frames contain broken, paint-spattered, dusty pieces of glass. (Anything with stained glass occupies a higher category and is bought by collectors with a different agenda and more cash.) I place the frames over a wide-mouth garbage can, glazed side down, and smash away with a hammer. Unadulterated therapy, especially at a time I'm feeling irritable or tense.

Next I remove all the remaining small pieces of glass and glaze compound, usually cutting away with a sharp chisel but sometimes using a propane torch to soften especially hardened putty. A propane torch. Macho. Very macho.

Oddly enough, it is the flaws, the scars in the wood, that most intrigue me. Each nick, each worn spot, reflects a story. I once acquired a set of large windows with thick wood running around and between six broken panes of glass. Under the center of the curving top piece all of the paint had been worn away, and the wood itself bore disfiguring gouge marks. Probably a school window, I thought, just like the ones in John Howland Elementary. We kids used to compete for the privilege of closing the high windows with a long pole that we balanced carefully and pushed up against the window frame, right under the middle of the top edge. How many children might have nudged this old window up and down as the seasons, and their lives, changed? When was the building it served torn down, and how long did it sit out in that salvage yard?

The experts now take over. First, a jaunt to the furniture-stripping place where all the remaining paint is removed in a chemical bath. I love this part. The removal of anywhere from one to five or more layers of thick paint suddenly reveals the raw wood in all its beauty, and for the first time I begin to feel a relationship with the person who crafted that window many years before. Occasionally I need to repair a lose joint or displaced mullion, and then there is a visit to the glass shop where individual mirror lights are carefully measured, then cut for each section and wrapped in paper for future installation.

Now comes the hard part, and also the most gratifying. Before I can insert the mirror sections and secure them with glazier's points, I must carefully prepare the wood and then coat it with rubbing wax or a lacquer. This process may involve extensive sanding of both small and large sections, some chiseling, and possibly burning off a leftover paint residue. The work can be tedious and on some projects painful when underused muscles are asked to perform unfamiliar tasks.

Still, there is a special satisfaction. I usually work in the cellar of our home except when using the propane torch; then I set up some sawhorses outdoors or, in winter, at least in the garage. But most often I find myself in front of the workbench, single bulb hanging overhead and only the radio and occasionally the dog or cat for company. It's at this point in each project, as I slowly and carefully prepare every square inch of wood, that I find myself connecting with the window's first builder, the person who, certainly decades ago and maybe much earlier, designed this window frame, cut the wood, prepared every contour, and invested his skill, his soul, into its production.

As the sanding of the wood and the removal of the last bits of paint and varnish return the window to its nakedness, I realize that I am looking at the same raw material that the first manufacturer saw. Beneath my hands is the original product, now ready to complete its transformation into a new object no doubt never considered by its maker. I would not go so far as to say that I feel a presence; but there certainly is a very clear acknowledgment that what I am doing, in some small way, recreates the spirit of long-dead carpenters as the work of their hands slowly reemerges into usefulness.

And now, the final steps. Varnishing the wood, careful insertion of the bright, clean pieces of mirror, and affixing kraft paper and a hanging wire to the back.

Finished. I prop the old/new object up on the workbench or against a wall and stare for a while, dabbing at a piece of dust clinging to the surface or smoothing a rough, splintery edge I had overlooked. And it is then, more than any other time, that I realize this is much more than a moderately lucrative hobby, more than a physical antidote to the purely intellectual endeavors that monopolize my life.

This is a rescue operation, a searching out and rehabilitation of pieces of strangers' lives, giving those battered, discarded creations a new function in which they become objects of interest, admiration, beauty.

I don't know if human beings are reincarnated. I'd like to think so, but lacking really credible witnesses, I can only view that particular option as one of several pleasant conjectures about what happens when life ends. Comforting, though, is the knowledge that with my own hands I can infuse new life and purpose into objects long cast off.

Sometimes one discovers holiness even in a musty basement workroom.

44. Two Lives, Two Triumphs

Frances Salmon was her name. I think it's all right to mention it. Apparently she had no relatives, few if any friends. She died, pretty much alone, about fifteen years ago.

My wife met Frances while making her social-work field placement rounds at a cancer hospital in Philadelphia. Sherri was assigned there as part of her M.S.W. training.

One of the oncologists had asked for a consult for Frances. She was profoundly depressed, and had every reason to be. Sixty-seven years old. Dying of breast cancer. Weak, in some pain, nearly totally dependent on the ministrations of strangers. Alone.

Sherri entered the room, introduced herself, and sat by the bed. After some polite conversation Sherri asked her usual question: "How can I help you?"

Frances explained that her pain was generally under control, and the doctors and nurses were very attentive. But she hated being in the hospital. Hated being ill. This was not how she had always envisioned the last part of her life.

Frances's complaints, Frances's depression, were all understandable. Sherri empathized with Frances, and on some issues helped her communicate her needs more clearly to her care providers.

After the surface issues had been addressed, Sherri changed the focus of her conversations with Frances. "Will you tell me who you are?" she asked. "Not just the woman here in the hospital bed. Tell me who you really are."

Frances was taken aback for a moment, almost puzzled at the request. Then she began to think. And to speak. And, eventually, to smile.

Later, with the subject's permission, Sherri wrote a paper about Frances. It was entitled "The Woman Who Rode Horses into the Sea."

Frances Salmon, cancer victim, terminally ill, helpless, was also the woman who rode horses into the sea. As she related to Sherri during their many visits, Frances had been a fabulous athlete, a daring, vivacious young woman who, for many summers, rode specially trained horses off the Steel Pier in Atlantic City. Frances was the woman whom thousands of people cheered as she and her horse took death-defying dives into the ocean. It was heart-stopping drama, and Frances was the absolute star.

Day after day patient and social worker spoke about Frances' extraordinary career. Eventually an album with photographs, newspaper articles, and handbills was added to the mix. Day by day Frances told the stories of her life. As she inevitably grew weaker, at the very same time she was helped to recreate herself as a person of unique accomplishment, understanding herself as the heroine that she truly was.

And that is how she died.

– ❖ –

I suspect that nearly every person harbors a triumph or two somewhere in their biography. Special acts, special moments. It may be a career of riding horses into the sea. It may be a fleeting instance of standing up to a fifth-grade bully. Earthshaking or absolutely mundane. No matter. What is important is how the memory of that triumph can grace one's life later on, when mustering inner reserves is the best response to dark times.

Like Frances Salmon, my special moment also involved horses. It's a story I adore telling, a piece of my life that I cherish.

It was the middle of August 1965. I was spending my fourth and final summer as a counselor at a southern New Hampshire camp called Tel Noar, Hebrew for "Hill of

Youth." I taught horseback riding. Not that I could ride. I could drive. That was the main qualification: someone who could drive the station wagon full of kids to the stables located a couple of miles from camp.

I drove the wagon and supervised the kids while the fifteen-year-old stable girl gave the so-called lessons.

My horse was called "Dusty." Had I named him, I would have thought up something far more creative, something like "Dr. Maurice J. Rabinowitz," but Dusty and I came to each other late in his life. In his youth he had been a sulky racer, and as such developed an unusually level trot. Though I didn't know much about horsemanship, I was able to cruise along on old Dusty, smooth as ice, and holler over to the kids who were bouncing sky high, "No. Just ride like I do. See? I'm not bouncing." They never caught on.

A few days prior to the conclusion of the season we always held a major all-camp competition, a brilliant concept that divided the kids into three teams and assured that fully two thirds of the children would return home as losers.

The start of the big event was never placed on the calendar; rather, some sort of "dramatic event" would take place to announce that the games or whatever had officially begun.

That's how it happened in the summer of '65. It was late in the afternoon, and the entire camp was gathered near the flagpole prior to dinner. All eyes were on Shirley Miller, the girls' head counselor, as she made the announcements of the day.

But something strange was occurring. The campers and the staff spotted him, though Shirley, whose back was to the large meadow, was unaware. Out of the meadow, riding a horse, came a sinister-looking figure, a man dressed in black with a bandanna covering his face and guns on either hip.

Too late to run! He took out a pistol, got the drop on poor Shirley, and (horror of horrors) forced her to surrender her symbol of authority, the silver whistle.

Shirley and the staff, and ultimately the kids, all began to panic as the evildoer stood by his horse, snarling a villainous snarl and admiring his newly acquired booty.

"The camp can't function without the whistle!" "All is lost!" "Oh, woe are we!"

Ah, but midst the depth of despair and gloom there was heard over the P.A. system the staccato trumpet call of the William Tell Overture: "Dum. Da-da-dum. Da-da-dum dum dum dum dum dum dum dum...." Familiar notes. Is it possible that...?

The kids standing to the left of the flagpole were the first to see. Fingers pointed, little ones jumped high to catch a glimpse, and soon everyone stared wide-eyed. For out of the far end of the meadow a lone horse and rider came racing, galloping toward the assembly. Cries of recognition and screams of delight were heard above the continued blaring of the music. "Da-da-dum, da-da-dum. Da da dum dum dum...."

And as the horse and rider drew closer, clods of earth flying off the swift hooves, it became apparent to everyone: The rider was a good guy. He was coming to rescue us all. He would save the camp.

He was Bob Alper.

I guided my sweating mount to a halt just a few yards behind the spot where the wicked intruder stood, still gloating over the stolen whistle and unaware of my approach. Pulling my gun, I got the drop on him, ceremoniously relieved him of the whistle, and returned it to Shirley as 350 pairs of hands acknowledged their rescuer, and 350 voices screamed in delight.

Following an unsmiling tip of my hat to the grateful

crowd, I ordered the thief to mount up. Then I took hold of Dusty's saddle horn, and without touching the stirrup, swung myself back into the saddle and the two of us headed off across the open grass.

On the far side of the meadow stood a small cabin. Once we reached it, we would turn and fade from sight.

As if the final moments of a well-choreographed ballet — and that is really what it was — we disappeared behind that cabin just as the final notes of the overture sounded in the distance.

What a delicious memory. It was theater. It was a young boy's fantasy come to life. It was a dream that actually happened.

Ten minutes later I found myself bailing macaroni and cheese onto plastic dinner plates and hoping that Joel Brody, excitable under any circumstances, would be able to retain his food at least until we had exited the dining hall. Yet I must admit, I was a bit of a hero that evening. A few admiring glances out of the corners of eyes. The little campers especially. I was pretty hot stuff. Until they assigned the kids and counselors to their respective teams, when suddenly I became a despised enemy to all those not on my side. By snack time, just before bed, the drama of late afternoon had been eclipsed by the thrill of newly formed unions and the contests that would begin the next morning.

Everybody seemed to have forgotten what I had done. But I remembered.

And I still do.

Thinking about that late afternoon ride always depresses me just a little, and cheers me a lot. What I realize is that I'll never be twenty years old again, galloping at breakneck speed across a meadow, the William Tell Overture's triumphal sounds filling the air. I'll never again rescue the damsel, save the multitude, and charge off into the sunset.

But I can dream. And I can recollect. And I can savor. Often, that's all I need.

Looking ahead, as many folks do, I hope for an easy death, a so-called good death in the company of a few people who may love me.

But if that is not to be, if somehow, some way, I find myself dying alone, like Frances Salmon — I just hope somebody will be there to listen to my story when I need to tell it.

SHERRIE NICKOL

About the Author

A native of Providence, Rhode Island, Robert A. Alper graduated from Lehigh University and was ordained as a rabbi at Cincinnati's Hebrew Union College – Jewish Institute of Religion in 1972. He served congregations in Buffalo and Philadelphia, and earned a Doctor of Ministry degree from the Princeton Theological Seminary. In 1986 he embarked on a parallel career as a stand-up comic, performing internationally. Alper is also the author of the color cartoon book *A Rabbi Confesses*.

He and his wife, Sherri, a psychotherapist, are parents of Zack and Jessie. They live in rural Vermont.